The Intuitive Trader

Developing Your Inner
Trading Wisdom

Robert Koppel

John Wiley & Sons, Inc.
New York • Chichester • Brisbane • Singapore

To my family
Mara, Lily, and Niko
and to my friend and business partner
Howard Abell

Copyright © 1996 by Robert Koppel
Published by John Wiley & Sons, Inc.

Library of Congress Cataloging-in-Publication Date:

Koppel, Robert.
     The intuitive trader : developing your inner trading wisdom for more successful trades / by Robert Koppel.
          p.   cm
     ISBN 0-471-13047-8 (cloth)
     1. Futures—United States.   2. Commodity futures—United States.
     3. Stockbrokers—United States—Interviews.   4. Intuition.
     I. Title
     HG6024.U6K673   1996
     332.64'5—dc20
                                                                      95-46089
                                                                         CIP

10   9   8   7   6   5   4   3

Every truth passes through three stages before it is recognized. In the first, it is ridiculed, in the second it is opposed, in the third it is regarded as self-evident.

—*Arthur Schopenhauer*

Contents

Foreword

William J. Brodsky, President
Chicago Mercantile Exchange

Although I am a lawyer by training, most of my professional life has been devoted to two of the nation's, indeed the world's, preeminent financial markets. For nearly a decade until 1982, I worked at the American Stock Exchange where I ultimately became executive vice president in charge of options, which back then were in their infancy. In 1982, I left Wall Street and headed West across the Hudson River to take a job at the Chicago Mercantile Exchange, where I have been president and chief executive since 1985.

Permit me to make two observations. New York and Chicago markets, once as different as a pork belly futures contract is from a share of stock, have converged in recent years and now share many basic functions and characteristics. Nonetheless, I would hasten to add, the cultures of the two markets, their respective customer bases, indeed the entire worldview of the rank-and-file of the two forums, remain separated by a considerable chasm.

Notwithstanding, there is a commonality shared by these two forums, a phenomenon that ties them together, squarely and ineluctably. That common denominator is the modern day trader, a market participant who, though always with us, has grown to nearly legendary status in recent years.

He or she can be found on the trading floors in New York or Chicago, or holed up in front of a computer screen in an upstairs office, or indeed, thanks to advanced telecommunications, in a cabin on a remote mountain aerie overlooking the Continental Divide. He trades in and out of the market with lightning speed and many times a day, seeking to make a profit, however small, by betting correctly on the future price move of everything from heating oil and lumber to interest rates, stock indices or a share of Microsoft stock. It is their presence in the market that gives our products their unalloyed, worldwide, and well-established reputation for liquidity.

Countless books and scholarly papers have been written about this market denizen. What makes him or her tick? What sets a successful trader apart from those who crash and go bust in the wake of a single, misguided, and costly bet on the future price move of the Standard & Poors 500 stock index, for example? What charts, candlestick configurations, weather patterns, or star alignments does the successful trader follow? What human qualities, traits, penchants of all kinds best dispose one to turning a market position into a winner? Or the reverse. What disposes such a market participant to failure, marks him or her for financial ruin, even?

Now comes Robert Koppel with his latest book, *The Intuitive Trader*. Koppel is no newcomer to the CME or to its markets or to writing books about traders and trading. Koppel and coauthor Howard Abell, a longtime friend and business partner, have exhaustively plumbed the traits, motivations, and modus operandi of successful traders in two previous books: *The Innergame of Trading* (Irwin, 1993) and *The Outer Game of Trading* (Irwin, 1994).

In his newest endeavor—this time a solo effort—Koppel explores a central paradox with which many industry traders in New York securities and Chicago futures and options markets are all too familiar. Although these market participants have been known to harbor an abiding appreciation and respect for the potential value this sixth sense, known as intuition, can bring to their professional lives, they rarely are able to identify it and confront it, much less bring themselves to act on it.

This inability, the author states, stems from personal conflicts, and more importantly, from biases weaving through a Western philosophical tradition that emphasizes a rational, empirical basis for action to the exclusion of such seemingly illusive considerations as intuition. To paraphrase Koppel, *The Intuitive Trader* provides a road map to developing the skill necessary to cultivate this vital sixth sense.

In Part III of his work, subtitled *The Top Traders*, Koppel provides us with interviews of four successful, rather widely known traders, all of whom are members of the CME and trade on its floor—Linda Leventhal, Howard Abell, Tom Belsanti, and Peter Mulmat. The comments of these "market wizards," as Koppel refers to them, provide a rare opportunity to hear firsthand how top market professionals use intuition in their professional lives.

There is no Rosetta Stone to trading or to any other profession where central mysteries, once unveiled, will take one necessarily down life's road to riches and fame, at the CME, the Amex, or any other financial market. That, of course, goes without saying.

But Koppel has written a book that, I must say, as a thirty-year veteran of both financial markets, cuts new ground in its exploration and exposition of intuition; in short, a "must read" for both the veteran and aspiring trader, whether fundamental or technical, long- term or short-, equity or derivative. Traders act on relevant information; that is a central tenet of their craft. In the following pages, Koppel provides new information—this time about a largely hidden aspect of human consciousness—that no doubt most traders will find as relevant and indispensable as a quote screen.

Bob Koppel is a pensive and erudite individual who studied philosophy and related disciplines in college and graduate school and later traded financial futures here at the CME. He has drawn heavily on these disparate backgrounds to produce a finished work that is as enjoyable to read as it is informative and entertaining.

Preface

The really valuable thing is intuition.

—Albert Einstein

In the *Intuitive Edge* (St. Martins, 1983), Philip Goldberg writes, "The more we know about intuition, the better equipped we are to use our own; the better our intuition the more we are in a position to understand it." Among traders intuition is a prized ideal, greatly sought after, though all too little understood. It is variously described by traders as a premonition, feeling, wish, impulse, hunch, awareness, belief, or state of mind. So, what exactly is intuition, and how can traders cultivate it to its full potential?

In the *Disciplined Trader* (NYIF, 1990), Mark Douglas observes, "A true intuitive impulse—a deeper level of knowledge and wisdom that will always indicate the next appropriate step to take—that will always be in our best interest, feels very much like wishing and hoping. In other words, it is very difficult to distinguish between the two, making it very easy to mix them up, which is one of the reasons why we find it so difficult to trust our intuition."

There are many reasons why it is difficult for traders to identify and then rely on their intuition. The reasons are paradoxical and unexpected, ranging from the personal to the cultural. The trader faces not only the natural conflicts present in his own makeup but the constraints of having to work within the rational empirical biases of the Western philosophical tradition, where long-standing epistemological assumptions have venerated rationalism and objectivity, largely discrediting the importance of intuition and "felt meaning" as a way of knowing.

Tony Saliba, one of the most successful equity options traders in the world, had this to say about the role of intuition when I interviewed him: "Intuition is ultimate market wisdom; knowing exactly what to do next, free of internal and external prejudice, having un-shakeable self-confidence and self-trust." Unfortunately, for most traders, reaching this level seems impossible. The primary reason for this has to do with ingrained psychological attitudes that allow us to negotiate successfully in the external environment but inhibit our performance in the trading (psychological) environment.

These attitudes include, but are not limited to, a need for certainty and control and an instinctive aversion to pain (losses). Developing the skills necessary for understanding intuition, and applying them to trading, provides proven ways to overcome these natural biases to produce measurable improvements.

A survey of recent titles focusing on "successful trading" (Schwager, *Market Wizards;* Douglas, *The Disciplined Trader;* Sperando, *Trader Vic*, etc., see "For Further Reading") reveal the importance of the trader's intuition, both from a psychological and strategic perspective; however, to date, no one has rigorously studied intuition or focused on how to develop intuition as a trading skill.

The Intuitive Trader provides an important blueprint to traders, enabling them to identify and learn how to cultivate the skills necessary to develop the intuitive sense. It also provides an opportunity to read how well-known market wizards apply intuition on an ongoing basis to their own trading. This is information that traders of various orientations, whether fundamental or technical, long- or short-term, equity or derivative, are eager to possess.

Success in trading!

–Bob Koppel

Acknowledgments

I wish to thank the traders and market experts who generously shared their ideas and insights into the workings of the intuitive mind; in particular, Howard Abell for his wealth of helpful suggestions, all of which were taken. I feel greatly enriched as a person to know Howard. He sets an exemplary standard as friend and business partner.

I would like to thank Mara Koppel for reading the original manuscript and for providing her fine editing. I am fortunate to have a wife who is an artist; twenty years of fascination with and love for the right hemisphere of her brain has prepared me well for writing this book.

Finally, I wish to thank Pam van Giessen and the staff at Wiley for their uncompromising support throughout this project.

Introduction

David Silverman, Director
Chicago Mercantile Exchange

In an interview with Jack Schwager in *The New Market Wizards* (Harper Business, 1992), Monroe Trout states that he could give the exact trading systems he uses to ten traders and some of them still wouldn't make money. Trout recognizes what all great traders know, that attaining profitability is not simply a mechanical endeavor but a creative, intuitive process.

Too often, traders lose sight of the key to success in trading. They convince themselves that success can be found in a head and shoulders pattern, a black box system (the more expensive, the better), or over the daily hotline of the latest trading guru. What these traders are forgetting or choosing to ignore is that successful trading begins and ends with self-awareness.

Most traders, particularly novices, resist this notion. Believing that trading is simply a game of numbers, of charts, prices, and profit and loss statements, they avoid the difficult task of self-examination. In *The Intuitive Trader*, Bob Koppel continues the work he began in his first two books with Howard Abell, *The Innergame of Trading* (Irwin, 1993) and *The Outer Game of Trading* (Irwin, 1994). In those works, he explains the psychological makeup of the successful trader. Using his extensive knowledge of and experience in the markets and through incisive and compelling interviews with top traders, he offers a blueprint for trading success that goes beyond the mechanical rules that most traders desperately want to believe is all that they need to know. In this current work, he expands on his original blueprint with a new goal in sight. He challenges the reader, through a series of interviews with top traders, to understand the differences between the left and right hemispheres of the brain. The left hemisphere serves to provide us with a framework for logical, rational, and objective analysis while the right hemisphere is a clearinghouse for our intuitive, creative, and subjective impulses. Koppel argues persuasively that using only the left hemisphere in the pursuit of trading success is limiting and self-defeating. The trader who takes command of the right hemisphere, however, is able to combine the practical with the artistic, the deductive with the inductive, and the intellectual with the intuitive.

The body of work being produced by Bob Koppel is well written, clearly presented, and, unlike many technical works on trading, within the intellectual capacity of the average trader. Throughout his writing runs the thread of simple common sense: in page after page, you will find yourself wondering why this point or that point never occurred to you. *The Intuitive Trader* is an important book that will remain fresh for years into the future, when the trading system you bought no longer works and when the guru has retired to Hawaii off the proceeds of his hotline. I encourage you to ask yourself the questions, consider the techniques, and read the interviews. I challenge you to become an intuitive trader.

PART I
THE INTUITIVE EDGE

Chapter One

The Intuitive Mind

Our duty to the world is to fulfill our individual potential.
> —*Stephen Spender, British essayist and poet*

Language—the primary tool of instruction—is itself largely a function of the left hemisphere of the brain. By definition, then, the workings of the right side of your brain can't be put into words as easily of those of the left side. . . . Yet even when the words escape us, we must remember the central point; the brain possesses an inherent capacity to change, a capacity which I've called the Principle of the Maximum Mind. You actually have the power to alter dramatically the way you think and act.
> —*Dr. Herbert Benson,*
> Your Maximum Mind *(Avon, 1987)*

In Michael Redman's latest movie *Il Postino* (*The Postman*), the internationally acclaimed writer Pablo Neruda is asked how does one become a poet? Neruda thinks for a moment and then in a flash his eyes brighten like a halogen lamp. His answer is simple: "You must walk beneath the cliffs of the Mediterranean, along its bays and beaches, and as you breath in the cool sea air begin to spontaneously generate metaphors!"

The great piano teacher Nadia Boulanger was once asked by one of her pupils if she thought he possessed the talent necessary to become a great pianist. Boulanger's answer too was simple: "When you wake up in the morning are your thoughts immersed in music? Are you surrounded by sounds and songs and rhythms until you yourself become music?"

It was Yogi Berra who said hitting is 90 percent mental and the other half is physical. I believe with some certainty that the same may be said of trading. Successful trading—that is, consistently profitable trading—involves far more than merely calling upon specific mechanical and strategic skills. It requires the development, cultivation, and conditioning of habits, thought patterns, and attitudes that influence the way we think and behave in the market. The toughest part of trading, in my view, is to overcome the rigid intellectual guardianship of the left brain, which serves to habituate existing behaviors and to rationalize the need for "logical consistency," and thus to emancipate the intuitive right side of our brain, the key to changing ingrained thought patterns and habits (see Figure 1-1). Many of our aesthetic abilities are rooted in the right side of the brain. We have all had the experience of a "flash" of thought or feeling, or a visual or auditory image that seemed to come right out of "nowhere," and as we were experiencing this "flash" we knew it was valid or true. "It just felt right." We have also had the opposite experience, and in fact, these experiences are embedded metaphorically in our language. We say something doesn't "smell," "taste," or "look" right. We also say that the story "sounded" fishy (there's a mixed metaphor) or that things "felt" wrong. We say the trade gave me a bad feeling "in my stomach." The key here is we arrived at this insight not through a logical or analytical process.

The right brain serves as a clearing house for our intuitive and

Figure 1-1   Characteristics of the Right and Left Hemispheres of the Brain

Left Hemisphere	Right Hemisphere
Analytic	Imaginative
Objective	Subjective
Deductive	Inductive
Timebound	Timeless
Scientific	Artistic
Conscious	Unconscious
Logical	Intuitive
Rational	Artistic
Intellectual	Feeling
Verbal	Metaphorical
Realistic	Internal

creative mental functions. As traders, the difficulty for most of us is that after we receive an intuitive impulse, these "messages from the beyond" are immediately dispatched to the left side of the brain for interpretation, selection, and analysis. We know the actual portion of the brain that performs this function. It is called the corpus callosum.

It must be remembered, of course, that the left brain performs an invaluable service for us. Without it, we could not function effectively as human beings: because of all the information that comes into our perceptual field from moment to moment, it is indispensable in determining, at any given point in time, what is important for us to know. Herbert Benson (*Your Maximum Mind*, Avon, 1987), sums up the dilemma well when he writes, ". . . Unfortunately, the left side of the brain is so important in its function that it has tended to overshadow the role of the right side of the brain. Yet the right side is the key to the plasticity of our minds, to our ability to change ingrained thought patterns and habits. It's the key to the operation of the principle of *Your Maximum Mind*. . . . The left side of the brain, with its powerful abilities to analyze and make convincing influences, may be portrayed as a kind of 'little dictator' over the right side. Many of our intuitive and creative functions, as well as much information that we need to know and use in changing our lives for the better, have in effect been enslaved by our rational left hemisphere. You might say we have become prisoner of the left side of our brains."

Traders need to be able to respond to information quickly and accurately from within in order to take effective action in the market. For many of us, changing existing trading habits, thought patterns, and attitudes—not accumulating new forms of technical analysis, or learning new indicators or systems—remains the most significant challenge. And it is not enough just to know this! Assiduous study is necessary but will not assure trading success. Our goal, therefore, may be characterized as an internal revolution of awareness that leads effortlessly to the adoption of unself-conscious action. As Benson puts it, "We must overthrow the hegemony of the left hemisphere and allow the right to break free and assume its full stature in the thinking process. In this way we can hope to open the door to beneficial change and growth in our lives."

The notion of felt meaning, that is, knowing something to be true

on a visceral level without applying exhaustive analysis or definition is well known and revered in the East. In the West, however,
unarticulated truth of a nonrational empirical basis has always been
regarded with skepticism at best and complete cynicism and rejec-
tion at worst. As traders, in my experience, most of what we do
when we're trading at our best in any moment of time is inexpress-
ible, beyond words and language, and can only be felt or imaged,
not described. Of course, after the experience, we can describe and
articulate the event and assign meaning. The important point here
is that the experience of successful trading is subjective, unself-conscious, and intuitive. This state of mind, it seems to me, has more
in common with the spirit of jazz—improvisational, automatic, and
responsive to the riff—than with a well-articulated and analyzed
process of decision making.

Remember the Samurai? These guys operated in a very physical
and dangerous context. Their sense of truth as it related to the per-
fection of their arts was life surviving and no nonsense. Their discipline was simple, spare, and natural. Their lives were spartan,
based not on the truth of doctrine, culture, or rarified learning but
on the unself-conscious, nonintellectual, responsive warrior mind
of action. Samurai training was founded on its unique understanding of the human mind and on what might be called the "mind's
inner truth reality."

The Samurai was involved in a disciplined process of deepening
and expanding his awareness until it permeated the total self and
governed every thought and action. Truth was existential and ex-
periential, not intellectual. Survival for the trader is just as real!

Every trader knows that market truth is existential not intellectual; its realization and practice are visceral, not cerebral. Inner market wisdom, like Samurai truth, is practiced truth that can only be
utilized and realized in action. It can never reside on the level of
mere theory.

One of the reasons it is so difficult to write about these issues in
a conventional way, and the reason I have chosen throughout *The
Intuitive Trader* to adopt a more conversational tone, is that my desire
is to circumvent your left brain in order to speak to your right hemisphere and to ask you for just this reading to suspend your normal
faculties of critical analysis and categorization. I believe that trading
at the highest levels of achievement, as with all expressions of peak

performance, is being in possession of the ability and freedom to act according to one's own inward perceptions and feelings of reality apart from the conventional wisdom, rules, and techniques of sound trading practices.

In *Zen and the Way of the Samurai, Arming the Samurai Psyche* (Oxford, 1993), Winston L. King writes, "The warrior, no matter how well trained in the techniques of his martial skills had to break through the superficial layers of his ordinary reasoning, his habit-ridden mentality, to the deeper center of his true original self."

In *Zen and Japanese Culture* (Princeton University Press, 1959), D. T. Suzuki describes the essence of the successful warrior. I believe it well describes the essence of being a successful and consistent trader. "However well a man may be trained in the art, the swordsman can never be the master of his technical knowledge unless all his psychic hindrances are removed and he can keep his mind in the state of emptiness, even purged of whatever technique he has obtained. The entire body together with the four limbs will then be capable of displaying for the first time and to its full extent all the art acquired by the training of several years. They will move as if automatically, with no conscious effort on the part of the swordsman himself. His activities will be a perfect model of swordplay. All the training is there but the mind is utterly unconscious of it."

We are left with a very difficult question: How is the trader then to overcome his ordinary reasoning, habit-driven behaviors, and self-defeating attitudes and move toward developing the psychological freedom to act upon his learned techniques in a visceral, unconscious, and intuitive way without the hamstrings of conscious fears or other mental hindrances? In other words: How is he to form a perfect blending of his mental powers of creative awareness and focus with his mechanical skills of execution?

It is my goal in *The Intuitive Trader* to answer this question, through narrative and interviews, by (1) establishing incontrovertibly the importance of trading in a state of mind where one's market actions are natural, unself-conscious, and automatic and (2) having the trader "know" viscerally the specific subjective elements that allow for an intuitive trading experience where one is prepared and available for enhanced personal performance.

Let us begin.

The great traders all hold one thing in common: they know exactly what they want to do in the market and possess the inner strength and will to do it. That's what separates them from the wannabes.

—Howard Abell

Chapter Two

Intuition and Successful Trading

I once had a philosophy professor who prefaced every lecture with the words "This is my truth." To be successful at trading, you have to find your own truth. *The Intuitive Trader* is my truth, and before I tell you more about my truth, I would like to tell you something about my background and training in order to let you know on what basis I have arrived at this truth.

I didn't start out to become a trader. In fact, I was trained as a student of philosophy at Columbia University where I concentrated on phenomenology and existentialism. For those of you who are not familiar with this branch of philosophy, it has to do with how we structure reality, both objective and subjective reality, and how we internalize that reality.

After I pursued this study for a number of years and conducted psychological research for a private institution, my wife, who is an artist with a keenly developed right brain and very intuitive sense of things, informed me that she had a burning desire for adventure. At this same time I felt my career in existentialism was at a dead end!

So I began looking around for other things to do. I visited my brother in Chicago, who at the time was trading in the bean pit at the Chicago Board of Trade. The first time I saw the trading floor, I experienced cannons going off. I was completely mesmerized by the atmosphere—a virtual Great Barrier Reef of human emotion and activity. Soon after, I became a floor trader and a member of the exchange, trading on the floor successfully for roughly fifteen years.

In addition to what I have already shared about my background, from 1990 to 1994 I participated in a very interesting experience with my close friend and business partner, Howard Abell. We interviewed some of the world's top traders. Our goal was to identify their inner psychology: What were they thinking at the point of trade analysis, selection, and execution? What was their own reality, that is, their subjective reality as it related to the market? And how did they process that information effectively? Our results were published in *The Innergame of Trading* (Irwin, 1993).

In a follow-up book, *The Outer Game of Trading* (Irwin, 1994), Howard and I studied how successful traders strategize, that is, how they put together their game plan. The idea was to learn how top traders formulate their strategy in much the same way as we might study the thinking of a grand master chess player, bracketing out any specific technical or methodological bias. I tell you these things to remind you that, as I stated earlier, this is my truth based on my orientation, educational background, and professional experience. I want to point out to you that what I am writing about here are all the issues that I feel must be addressed in order to become an intuitive trader, which I believe, based on my experience and interviews with some of the world's most successful traders, is the take-off point for developing the internal skills of trading mastery.

I invite you to take part in this process as if it were a seminar or workshop. Particularize the issues as I write about them. In short, join me as an active participant on this journey.

When we were kids and it was a rainy day and there was a puddle in front of us, we used to jump right into the center of that puddle. Remember how good that felt! Today we have a tendency to dismiss the great fun of puddles and tiptoe around them. Now I encourage you to play with me. Sometimes the issues may seem abstract. Challenge yourself with a specific example of how these issues affect you. See and hear them in your own mind. Feel how they relate to your own trading. See how the issues of motivation, belief, and state of mind relate to your own market experience.

As we move forward, bring into clear focus the times that you were right in the market, yet you hesitated, or the times you stayed too long in a position and it went bad. Remember the time you just felt that you had to capture the profit too soon, or the time you were just wondering to yourself, what in the hell is going on! Have you ever had that experience? I have and so have many of the traders I have interviewed. In short, I ask you to adopt an attitude of commitment over resignation, control over powerlessness, and challenge over threat as we begin to investigate the relationship between intuition and successful trading.

I want to ask you a question. What do you believe are the shared characteristics of successful traders?

If we were to generate a list of those qualities and characteristics that the top traders hold in common, I think we would all agree, it would look something like this:

Confident	Organized
Disciplined	Goal-oriented
Self-reliant	Self-contained
Motivated	Knowledgeable
Competent	Open-minded
Self-aware	Determined
Optimistic	Enjoying trading
Intuitive	Risk managing
Honest	Focused
Strategic	Independent
Patient	Ambitious
Hard-working	Committed
High achieving	Managing stress
Energetic	Automatic
Objective	Risk-taking
Proactive	

If we would then attempt to make specific statements about exactly what separates the best from the rest of the pack, I think you too would agree with the following:

1. They understand their motives for trading.
2. They develop trading strategies that work for them because they fit their personalities.
3. They enjoy trading and make it effortless.
4. They work hard at developing their skills and maintaining a trading edge.
5. They trade with total confidence in themselves and their methodology.

6. They trade in a positive state of mind that allows them the flexibility to act automatically and know exactly what is the next right step to take.
7. They intuitively understand money management and risk control and "know" that no single trade is worth not being able to trade tomorrow.
8. They have a strategy that works and the discipline to carry it forward.
9. They are independent minded and understand that they are personally responsible for all market decisions.
10. They understand the difference between loss and losing.
11. They understand the importance of acting at difficult times with circumscribed risk.
12. They know what drives markets and what is the difference between hope and fear.
13. They don't trade to please others.

As you look at these two lists, ask yourself this question: Do you believe you possess these qualities and characteristics? Unless you strongly believe that you can develop them, you are surely pursuing the wrong path. As a friend of mine is fond of saying, "Believing is seeing."

If you don't see yourself, in a literal sense, and feel yourself possessing these qualities, characteristics, and attitudes, you will not sustain the effort, commitment, and hard work that is required to achieve peak performance as a trader or in anything else. As I pointed out in *The Innergame of Trading*, what you believe about yourself and the market will enhance or inhibit your performance with dramatic results. In *Unlimited Power* (Fawcett, 1986), Anthony Robbins writes, "Our beliefs about what we are and what we can be precisely determine what we will be. If we believe in magic, we'll live a magical life. If we believe our life is defined by narrow limits, we've suddenly made those limits real. What we believe to be true, what we believe is possible, becomes what's true, becomes what's possible."

Intuitive trading, that is, flawless execution of one's proven market techniques, grows in the soil of hard work, discipline, and preparation. Becoming an intuitive trader requires an ongoing commitment to mastery, to overcome internal hindrances and fears. John R. Noe observes in *Peak Performing Principles for High Achievers* (Berkeley, 1984), "Fear is the most powerfully inhibiting force known to man. It restricts us, tightens us, and causes us to panic, forcing us to abandon our great plans of life. If we are not willing to do what we fear, the fear, not ourselves, is in control of our lives. The high achiever can not afford to surrender control of his or her life to fear."

There is an anecdote that is told of H. L. Mencken who on a particularly quiet day in an otherwise noisy newsroom began to shout at the top of his lungs, "It's coming in the doors, we must stop it!" Needless to say, everyone stopped what they were doing and began looking in his direction.

"It's up to the bottom of the desks!" yelled Mencken and then he shouted again, "It's up to the seats of our chairs!"

Mencken's colleagues began to look at one another, and seeing no observable threat, they began to mutter among themselves, "What the hell is he talking about?" In a final grand gesture Mencken jumped on top of his desk and bellowed, "Mediocrity! We're drowning in mediocrity!"

Commitment to hard work and self-improvement may seem to be an obvious point; however, in reality I believe it's the essential point. It is what provides the personal propulsion toward excellence and the means with which we grow to learn more about ourselves. Commitment is the psychic fuel that allows us to face our fears, to realize we cannot escape them, that to face them is to overcome them. The importance of this lies in the all-too-familiar saw that the power of fear is amplified by fear itself. If we don't confront our fears in trading or anything else, what results is an experience that is based on intimidation, wasted potential, and pessimism.

To overcome the fear, you must face it head on because if you don't control the fear, as I stated earlier, it will control you. I once heard Zig Ziglar define fear in a most memorable way: "Fear is an acronym; it stands for False Evidence Appearing Real."

As you begin to think about the internal hindrances and fears that are keeping you from achieving the result you want in the market, ask yourself the following questions. (Yes, really write down the answers.)

1. Do I really want to become a successful trader? Why?

2. Do I possess the internal skills necessary to succeed?

3. What really matters most to me?

4. Am I willing to pay the price?

5. Am I willing to assume responsibility for all my actions?

6. Am I willing to start where I am?

7. Am I willing to think for myself?

8. Am I committed to living up to my full potential?

Some folks think traders have a nice life, based on the misbegotten notion that they breeze in at about 8:30 in the morning and are out the door and on the golf course or wherever by 1:00 or 2:00 in the afternoon. What they don't realize is how much happens before and after the opening and closing bells. Just as any trial lawyer worth his or her salt devotes many, many hours to preparation and strategy, so does any good trader. Preparing for those crucial hours on the floor entails an incredible amount of homework: no chart is ignored, no statistic, however esoteric it may seem, is discounted. Next, a precise strategy for the next day's trading must be mapped. That strategy must be so thorough that it will get the trader into the market at exactly the right point, define the trader's risk, and take the trader out at just the precise moment. Once on the floor, it should all be a matter of focus and execution.

—*Jack Sandner*
Chairman, CME

Intuition and Strategy

"Think of what is right and true. Learn to see everything accurately. Become aware of what is not obvious. Be careful even in small matters. Do not do anything useless." This was the advice of Miyamoto Musashi in the *Book of the Five Rings* (1643). It is one of the most important Samurai texts ever written. Its strategic insights were designed for leaders in all professions who were searching for individual mastery and personal excellence.

The curious fact about Musashi's advice, and for that matter, all recommendations about successful trading practice is that in a real and practical sense, *strategy* and *technique* must be learned only to be forgotten. It is not my intention to be cute when I say that. What I mean is that you must work hard at learning an effective technique and strategy, but this is only a starting point. It is like becoming a jazz musician. You must spend countless hours practicing, doing scale work and fingering exercises, but when you are truly playing, you must be prepared to let go and follow where the line takes you, to be immersed in the spirit and soul of the music.

In *Zen and the Way of the Sword, Arming the Samurai Psyche* (Oxford, 1990), Winston L. King underscores this point: "The swordsman handles his sword as if he were handling chopsticks, picking up a piece of food and putting it into his mouth. . . . Everything must be turned over to the unconscious/subconscious visceral awareness. There is no room or time here for thought."

I believe Ed Seykota, a market wizard, made this same point when he was interviewed by Jack Schwager. Seykota indicated there are five trading rules he lives by:

1. Cut losses.
2. Ride winners.
3. Keep bets small.
4. Follow the rules without question.
5. Know when to break the rules.

But what exactly is it that we have to learn about trading strategy before we forget it? I believe the following list represents the essential elements of a successful strategy.

- Assumes personal responsibility for all market actions.
- Takes into consideration your motivation for trading.
- Allows you to trade to win.
- Establishes goals and formulates a plan to take action.
- Controls anxiety.
- Creates a point of focus.
- Is consistent and congruent with your personality.
- Allows you to have an edge.
- Manages risk and assumes losses.
- Is profit oriented and practical.
- Identifies opportunities and leaves no uncertainty.
- Allows for patience and trading in a resourceful state of mind.

Assumes Personal Responsibility for All Market Actions. You are at the controls. All market decisions and actions begin and end with you. As the well-known saying goes, "Don't complain and don't explain." The good thing to remember is you get all the credit.

Takes into Consideration Your Motivation for Trading. People trade for a variety of reasons. Many of the reasons traders have for trading impede rather than enhance performance. You must know viscerally and intellectually why you want to trade and what you are willing to do to achieve your goals.

Allows You to Trade to Win. As I've said many times before, "Most traders do not trade to win, they trade not to lose. You must trade full out—to buy automatically at your numbers, to catch breakouts and to enter and exit at your signals. You must be prepared to step into puddles without taking a bath!

Establishes Goals and Formulates a Plan to Take Action. In *The Innergame of Trading* I wrote extensively on the relationship between successful trading performance and goal setting (see Figure 1-2). In short, goal setting does the following:

- Identifies what is important to you.
- Increases motivation.
- Directs your focus.
- Identifies relevant trading strategies and skills.

Figure 1-2   The Importance of Trading Goals

Goal	Benefit	Trading Behavior
Performance goal	Focuses on improvement in relation to your own standards.	Increases physical and psychological skills related to trading.
Outcome goal	Helps to determine what's important to you.	Allows for the development of techniques and strategies that match your personality.
Motivation goal	Helps to increase effort, direct attention.	Allows traders to maintain a high level of enthusiasm and confidence.

It should also be remembered that when setting goals, the goals should be

- Specific—clear, precise, well defined
- Time framed
- Positive—stated in a way that empowers
- In your control
- Realistic
- Measurable—easily quantifiable

The more you can see, hear, and feel yourself accomplish your goal through vivid visual, auditory, and kinesthetic (feeling) imagery, the greater is your chance of achieving your ultimate objective.

In my experience the factors that prevent traders from achieving their trading goals are these:

- Self-limiting beliefs
- Poor focus
- Ill-defined personal strategy
- Lack of physical and psychological energy
- Unresourceful state of mind

Controls Anxiety. We are barraged as traders with a variety of anxieties that we must learn how to manage (see Figure 1-3). A well-planned strategy minimizes the role of anxiety by addressing the factors that produce these feelings (loss, risk management, market entry and exit, etc.).

Figure 1-3   Sources of Trading Anxiety

Anxiety	Manifestation of Trading Behavior
Fear of failure	Trader feels intense pressure to perform, ties self-worth to trading, strives for perfection. Trader is concerned about what others think.
Fear of success	Trader loses control, engages in euphoric trading. Trader doubts himself.
Fear of inadequacy	Trader experiences loss of self-esteem, diminished confidence.
Loss of control	Trader loses sense of personal responsibility when trading. Trader feels market is out to get him.

Creates a Point of Focus. This is an essential point, and it is tied to the whole issue of market reality (more about this later). You must know what you are personally looking for and at in the market. That's really all that matters! Being able to do this enables you to distinguish

- The signal from the noise
- High-probability from low-probability trades
- Risk controlled from out-of-control trades

Is Consistent and Congruent with Your Personality. Your strategy must "feel good." It must be automatic, effortless, and decisive in its implementation. Ask yourself the following questions:

1. What are my weaknesses as a trader?
2. What are my greatest strengths as a trader?
3. What do I find most interesting about trading?
4. What do I find least interesting about trading?
5. What do I find most enjoyable about trading?
6. What do I find least enjoyable about trading?
7. How much time, effort, and money am I willing to commit to trading?

8. Is it important for me to trade by feel? Why?
9. Is it important for me to have a totally mechanical system? Why?
10. What does my ideal trading system look like?

Being able to answer these questions allows you to develop trading tactics and strategies that conform to your unique personality. Remember, trading strategies do not come off the rack, with one size fitting all. If it's going to work, it must feel natural.

Allows You to Have an Edge. The idea of having an edge in the market is greatly related to the notion of having your own point of focus and creating a trading system that feels "right." Your ultimate edge is tailoring your strategy to your subjective "take" on the market. Your execution skills, therefore, must be developed to allow you to react decisively as your signals click in. The market gives you no edge. Edge is created by your reaction and responsiveness to what the market reveals.

Manages Risk and Assumes Losses. Some traders are still of the opinion that we "make" profits and "take" losses. The simple answer is: we make both. Loss has to be assumed in trading as inevitable not accidental. Taking a loss is not doing something wrong. In fact, it is doing something right! It is a constant that all successful traders have in common: they take losses. It should be obvious that good risk management assumes that no single loss will ever get out of hand.

Is Profit Oriented and Practical. This point may seem obvious, although in my experience in working with traders, it is not. Many traders expect the market to conform to their theoretical notions or technical bias. The name of the game is performance. Only after you understand this fact can you learn how to become an intuitive trader.

Identifies Opportunites and Leaves no Uncertainty. According to Anthony Robbins, "The difference between those who succeed and those who fail isn't what they have—it's what they choose to see and do with their resources and experiences of life." This also applies to trading. Your strategy provides the organization and focus for you to identify opportunities in order to act with decision and consistency. In addition, it allows you to "know" what is the next right step to take in the market. Think in probabilities, trade with certainty.

Allows for Patience and Trading in a Resourceful State of Mind. Once the trade is made, your strategy must allow you to remain calm, patient, resourceful, and focused. It is the ability to do this on an ongoing basis, no matter what the market throws your way, that will enable you to be open and available to your creative and intuitive impulses as a trader. Trading in a resourceful state of mind is the key to becoming an intuitive trader.

Let's now turn to the experts and top traders and see how they understand the relationship between intuition and trading.

While being trained in the art, the pupil is to be active and dynamic in every way. But in actual combat, his mind must be calm and not at all disturbed. He must feel as if nothing critical is happening. His steps are securely on the ground, and his eyes are not glaringly fixed on the enemy. His behavior is not in any way different from his everyday behavior. No change is taking place in his expression, nothing betrays the fact that he is now engaged in mortal combat.

—*Suzuki (1959)*

The markets are the same now as they were five or ten years ago because they keep changing—just like they did then.

—*Ed Seykota*

PART II
THE MANY FACES OF INTUITION

Chapter Three

Bill Williams, Ph.D.

Bill Williams is the founder of the Profitunity Trading Group and has been actively trading for over thirty-five years. His innovative work into the physics of consciousness produced a new way of looking at psychotherapy and the interaction between the trader's psyche and the market. Dr. Williams is the developer of the Market Facilitation Index (M.F.I.), which is now standard on many analytical computer programs worldwide, and is the discoverer of the fractal of the Elliott wave.

Dr. Williams is recognized as the foremost active trader using fractals and the science of chaos. He is the author of the recently published book Trading Chaos, Applying Expert Techniques to Maximize Profits *(Wiley, 1995).*

Q: Bill, what first attracted you to trading?

Bill: I was teaching at a university and down the hall from me was an accounting professor who was trading stocks. He seemed to be making more money on the side from trading than he did as a professor. At first, I was basically shadowing him, and I should say he was quite good! Of course, this wasn't good for me. It gave me a false sense of security. You see, it made me think I was good while in actuality I was just following him.

Q: So in the early years of your trading, what was your performance like? What do you think was the most important thing you learned from your early experience?

Bill: Well, to tell you the truth, looking back on it during those early years, I'm not sure I learned a whole hell of a lot. I was actually extremely lucky! And looking back on it today, I probably should have gone bankrupt several times over! I think I was lucky because I wasn't paying a great deal of attention to the market. This was still before I went from trading stocks to trading commodities.

Q: Why did you start trading commodities?

Bill: I was the executive vice president of the largest carpet manufacturing company in the world. Our stock suddenly took a big leap up, for what appeared to be no reason at all, except that some insider information kind of propelled the stock sky high. This really scared me away from stocks and sent me toward commodities. I was convinced futures were a much more level playing field. When I really started trading futures full time, I did not do well at all. I sat bell to bell in front of the monitor full time every minute that the market was open and could not figure out why I wasn't doing well. This was particularly puzzling for me because I did pretty well as an amateur and figured I should do twice as well as a professional full-time trader. But as I said, the results were just the opposite. I did not do well at all until I finally realized, and here comes the answer to your second question, I had this big realization and what I realized was nobody trades the market! Everybody trades their own personal belief system!

Q: With your background in psychology, were you thinking at this time about the relationship between psychology and one's trading performance?

Bill: Not exactly, but I did realize that after spending a few sleepless nights over some losses.

Q: That does have a way of capturing your attention.

Bill: Yes. I realized that the losses were not only upsetting my sleep pattern but were upsetting the entire grace of my life.

Q: Could you be more specific, Bill?

Bill: I mean it was affecting my relationship with my family and everything else. And, I should add, I was convinced at that point that it wasn't worth it. That either I had to get on a better track or I had to give the whole thing up.

Q: You spoke a moment ago about belief systems. And what I want to ask is that when you started trading, did you have that notion in mind based on your background and training? In other words, was your initial trading methodology idiosyncratic, or was it pretty much following an objective system?

Bill: Well, yes and no. As I said, I was not putting much time into my trading. There was no uniformity and there was no real order to it at all. It was pretty much just kind of cherry picking, unfortunately lucky cherry picking. But again, as you point out, my background and training in graduate school was on the mind-body connection. I had a grant from the University of Miami medical school and developed a body-centered psychotherapy that we called the "physics of consciousness." What we were doing was relating how thinking and feeling affects the body and how the body affects thinking and feeling in performance. I was very involved in this work.

Q: Did your initial market experience make you see the need to incorporate some of your mind-body work into your trading strategy?

Bill: Not at first. In fact, initially I ignored that background because I looked at the market as a kind of logical financial network and thought that all you have to do is just figure out how it works, and you add up the figures and you're ready to go!

Q: It's interesting how we all do that. I've noticed that some of the most successful traders, no matter if their background was in music or psychology or architecture or athletics, during their novice experience reject all the knowledge and training that preceded the trading. Only when they begin to focus on what it was that made them successful in that other area of their interest do they begin to really get good results in the market. So am I correct in stating that this is consistent with your experience as well, Bill?

Bill: Absolutely parallels it! Once I think I realized that one of my errors was an error in logic. I was trading the market the same way I would go out and buy a car. And to give you a sense of what was happening, I was paying serious attention to things that were being written in *The Wall Street Journal* and reported as news items on FNN, not really realizing that trading commodities and stocks is really a fantasy game. I mean this in the sense that you're trading future utility and you're trying to figure out how to anticipate the anticipators. You're trying to figure out where the market is going to be six months from now. And that makes it a much more level playing field. But it takes you totally out of the realm of traditional logic, in my opinion. From this point of view, you or I or anybody else can have an equally good guess as to what the market is going to do this summer. The point I'm trying to make is I had to transfer my entire thinking process and move from conventional logical formulations to thinking in terms of future utility.

Q: So how did you begin to build this concept into your current trading methodology?

Bill: I was really motivated by a feeling of desperation. I'm not kidding! I had a recurring nightmare that I was going to have to go out and get a real job.

Q: Oh.

Bill: And I didn't want to do that! So I was basically trying out any kind of idea or concept that I thought would work. And I guess I came to my solution through a process of elimination. Through trial and error I eliminated everything that would work or was told would work but didn't work and finally realized that everybody trades only one thing: their own belief system. No trader, whether an institution or whatever, trades an objective market. We all trade what we believe.

The second big realization for me was how simple trading the market really is. I realized that the whole purpose of the market is to find that particular spot where there's an equal disagreement on value and an agreement on price. And since I realized that assumption is true, it helped me to simplify my trading a great deal. For example, I immediately threw out bullish and bearish consensus. Today, for example, I absolutely do not believe that there's any such thing as an oversold or overbought condition! I think my trading improved dramatically the simpler I thought. The more things of an educational, logical, or sophisticated nature that I got out of the way, the better my results.

Q: Was there a defining experience for you, Bill?

Bill: Yes. Almost going broke.

Q: That's very defining.

Bill: Yes. Seriously. My net worth was reaching a critical point.
It got down to where it was very serious. If I wanted to keep trading, my trading had to improve!

And I was spending an awful lot of money trading. In fact, the first month I started trading full time, I spent over $6000 just on newsletters, figuring that the guys who were writing these newsletters knew more than I. That $6000 ended up costing me well over $100,000.

Q: In your opinion, Bill, what are the characteristics of a successful trader?

Bill: I think there are a couple of characteristics that are essential. First and foremost, it's very important that a trader be in touch with himself. The second important attribute for a trader is to be brutally honest with yourself. You can't take your trading results and jack them up and glaze them over on yourself. You've got to see the market for what it is. I know some traders who, for example, when they get a bad Profit and Loss statement refuse to open the envelope! They'll hide it away in a drawer. But, if they get a good one, they want to go brag to their wives and kids and anyone else who will listen.

It is also critical, I believe, to get the left hemisphere of your brain, the ego and the conscious mind, out of the way. You see, in my view, trading is much more like riding a bicycle than doing a mathematical exercise.

Q: Bill, what you are saying then is that trading at the highest level is more a right-brain activity than a left-brain activity?

Bill: Absolutely. From a psychological standpoint, Bob, I think there are two fundamental functions of the left hemisphere. The first function I think we should talk about is the left hemisphere's role of habituating existing behavior. For example, when you're learning to ride a bicycle, you have to think about it an awful lot. And then over time as you habituate the riding to your unconscious or right hemisphere, you don't have to think about it anymore. Just as you didn't have to think about how you dried off this morning after showering or how you shaved. You learn more and more about trading, and the ideal thing is to be able to forget and let go and just do it.

The second function of the left hemisphere that really screwed me up, and I think screws up a lot of traders, is its problem-solving function. For example, you come into trading to solve the problem that you don't have enough money and you get very lucky and you make a lot of money. Well, you don't have as much of a problem, so your tendency is to not work as hard as you did before. You tend to quit doing the things that made you successful in the first place.

Let's say you're eighty pounds overweight and you lose ten pounds. Those first ten pounds are pretty easy. At seventy pounds overweight, maybe you're not quite as uncomfortable, nor are you as motivated to lose weight as when you were eighty pounds overweight. So again the idea here is that as soon as you start to become successful, you tend to quit doing the very thing that gave you the results you desired.

I think the key is to use both functions of the left brain to your advantage. You've got to use both functions. You've got to let the left hemisphere habituate your successful trading behavior first, and second you've got to get out of the problem-solving mode!

Q: Bill, I think that is quite right. I also have found that traders who are functioning at the highest level are operating in the market on an almost purely aesthetic level. It seems to me it is almost entirely a right-brain rather than a left-brain activity.

Bill: Well, that certainly has been my personal experience. And my experience has been confirmed through my association with some very good traders.

Q: Bill, let me ask you another question. In your opinion, what are the specific stages that traders go through before they can trade on an intuitive level?

Bill: Good question. I think that in learning any activity there are five stages. I think one of the real problems in trading is that there are so few places to go to learn how to do it right. There's no Little League, no training wheel, no grammar school: when you start a small account, you can trade a bond and now you're immediately in competition with the best bond traders in the whole world. You're in the championship ring! But to answer your question specifically, there are five levels. The first level, and I should add that these are obviously not original, is the novice level.

At the novice level, basically, you're just learning how things work. You're learning the vocabulary. The goal is to stay in the market while you gain experience, and this will all be important later on because trading is both a science and an art. And the art is developed only after a great deal of experience. At this novice level, your job plain and simple is to gain experience and not to lose money.

At the second level, you take a different point of view. For example, if we were talking about playing the piano, at the first level you would be learning what the notes are; at the second level, you'd start putting notes together. So in trading, you start putting trades together so that you learn how to make a profit consistently on a one-contract basis.

The third level is what I call a competent level. Remember, at the first level you're trying to tread water. At the second level you're trying to make money on a one-contract basis. On the the third level your goal is consistently to maximize your rate of return on your capital. At level three you're trading multiple contracts, spreads, options, all kinds of derivatives, and everything else.

In my judgment, the real transition occurs when you move past the competent level. I think the biggest jump of all in trading is between the third and fourth levels, between the competent and what I call the proficient level. You see, the reason the difference between these two levels is so significant is that in the proficient level, you're really putting yourself into your trading in a very real and personal way. You become part of the market.

It's as if you're a surfer and you're going out and you just intuitively know where that big wave is coming from and how you should ride it and zig and zag with it in a way that is effortless and natural. In music, at the competent level you play music, which is to say you play the music exactly as it's written. But truthfully, you're no better than a player piano at that level.

Q: You're playing it mechanically.

Bill: It's mechanical. It's not you! You're reading the music and you may be reading it perfectly, but there's none of you in there. In trading, you're reading the market, and you may know what it's going to do, but you are not personally and intuitively involved.

Q: What's different on the fourth level?

Bill: At the fourth level, it is you! So if I were playing the piano, I would not play it exactly as it's written. I would play it to put more of my own feeling or interpretation or intuition into it. I might hold a note a little longer, or if I were singing, I might be a little flat or sharp or whatever. But the playing or singing becomes more of a reflection of me!

At this level you know what is the right trade without knowing how you know. There's no prodding to get into the trade. You see the trade, and you automatically take it. It's just the automatic thing to do. No hesitation!

At the fifth level, which is what I call the expert level, trading is almost all right hemisphere. It's all intuitive. It's all feeling. And I should add, I believe that's a characteristic of expert performance in athletics or in any field.

Q: I know that in your workshops you refer to level five as being all state of mind.

Bill: Yes.

Q: And that . . .

Bill: Trading becomes the ability to constantly refocus your state of mind.

Q: Are you saying then, Bill, that at level five, trading the market becomes an exercise of monitoring how you're thinking and feeling at any given moment, what you're seeing, how you're representing that experience to yourself?

Bill: Exactly! And with that realization the entire character of trading changes. You see, your focus becomes not to make money but to find out who you are and what you are experiencing in the market to allow yourself to achieve consistency. As I often say, trading becomes the most naked psychotherapy in the whole world!

Q: Now that's a good way of putting it.

Bill: It is! I've often said that if you really are interested in getting enlightened, one way would be to go off to Tibet, crawl in a cave, and sit there meditating for thirty years. Another equally good way—but much, much faster—is to trade the S&P and rigorously focus on what you are thinking and feeling.

Q: Well, yes, the S&P will teach you very quickly how you value yourself and how you "choose" to represent your market experience to yourself.

Bill: Of course, that is one of the most crucial things. For example, in our experience working with traders in private tutorials, most of them come in with a statement like, "The market stopped me out" or some other statement that this or that was inflicted on them. Hopefully when they leave, they realize that the market didn't do anything. Tracy, my assistant, has a saying that he's going to put up over his monitor. It reads: "It's all my fault." And he's right. He's absolutely right!

Q: You know, if you think about anything that you do in life to the extent that you have control over it, your feelings of self-evaluation are pretty high. But as soon as you feel a victim to external circumstances (i.e., the market), your self-esteem goes down, and consequently, your performance suffers.

Bill: Absolutely! I think athletics is a very good analogy. Athletes talk about getting in the zone and getting in the "flow." There's a book by a guy up in Chicago whose name I cannot pronounce.

Q: Yes, I know. I speak about his (Mihaly Czikszentmihalyi) work with my traders.

Bill: One of the concepts he puts forward very clearly is that one of the crucial aspects to getting in the state of mind, which as I said before is critical at the fourth and fifth level, is that you must have control and immediate feedback and you really must enjoy what you're doing. He talks about brain surgeons who enjoy their work so much that they go on vacation and do brain surgeries in Third World countries. He says that one of the keys to this flow's fate is immediate feedback. When they cut into a brain, they know immediately, every second they're operating, whether they're doing well. I think this same kind of thing happens in the market when you're trading. If you know how to pay attention (level four and five), you know immediately how it's going for you. I think when we use this feedback we learn how to let go. I think "letting go" is really much more important than almost anything else in trading. And, as you know, Bob, I have been working on an article based on the view that the more intelligent you are, the more difficult it is to make money in the market initially. You have a tendency to out think the market and possess the fear of "letting go"; you're afraid to go with the flow. Relying on your own intuition becomes a source of anxiety.

Q: I think, in a very practical sense, you are right. Both you and I have seen that some of the most talented technical and fundamental analysts tend to make the worst traders.

Bill: Absolutely. In fact, I would venture a guess that if it were possible to rank all the commodity analysts in the world, ranking them by brilliance and intelligence, you wouldn't find a winning trader in the top 30 percent!

Q: True. Bill, if you could focus specifically on the issue of intuition, most people think of it as being the ability to look into the future or possess some faculty like ESP. From your perspective, what is intuition? And how does it relate to trading?

Bill: Let me preface my answer by saying that I am very committed to the new science of chaos for a number of reasons. I think it has changed my life. I'm certain it has improved my trading. One of the characteristics of chaos is that it provides a new way to perceive information. It provides a perspective on any type of organization, no matter what it is, whether it's straightening out the socks in your drawer or arranging your desktop or, for that matter, trading in the market. Any attempt at organization of any sort is a resistance to chaos.

Now from this point of view, chaos in a literal sense is more than the unfolding or recovery of "new information." What happens is you resist chaos and what you build is some kind of form. And it doesn't matter whether we're talking about something that is psychological or physical or chaotic. Anytime you have a form, that form, of necessity, wants to perpetuate itself.

Q: Can you give me an example of that?

Bill: I can give you several examples. Let's take the chair you're sitting in. It is a chair and it's hard and it wants to perpetuate itself. Or consider all those people who want to do away with the IRS. That's going to be one hell of a job because the IRS too wants to perpetuate itself!

Q: How do you vote on that one?

Bill: I'm for getting rid of it. I want more chaos. The four biggest moneymakers in the world are war, insurance, medicine, and religion. And the thing that's interesting about this is that they all have to do with our fear of death. It's all based on a fear of death, and the fear of death is nothing more than trying to promulgate our current form.

Q: Are you talking about the Darwinian idea of self-preservation?

Bill: Yes. Preservation of the species is a resistance to chaos. We have all these anecdotal reports about people who have near-death experiences: that it's beautiful and it's wonderful and no longer do they fear death and this kind of thing. I think there's probably something to that.

In the market what all this means is that when you're in the sideways or bracketed market, it usually goes on interminably longer than you think it's going to. And when you're in a good trend, it too will go on longer than anybody thinks. It literally has a need to perpetuate itself.

Q: Why then is it so hard for traders to perpetuate profits when they're in a good trade?

Bill: Assuming that we're right in our concept that chaos is new information, when new information comes into your perceptual field, you have to deal with it in some way. And, again, new information can be the bonds or S&P's ticking up or whatever. There's a psychological theory that says anytime you feel overwhelmed or bored, it's because you're trying to put new incoming information into old categories. Of course, it is very interesting to think about trading in this light. Let me give you a specific example. Let's say that we have two atoms. One atom is the hydrogen atom, a very simple little organization that has a proton and an electron. And this hydrogen atom is a gas. It's floating around the room just as free as a bird. It comes in contact with an oxygen atom. And the oxygen atom has an unstable electron in its orbit. Now, in the atom, the nucleus would be you and the electron would be your belief systems. So you come in contact with something else that has a different sort of belief system, if you will. And that atom has a choice. It has a decision to make. The choice it makes the vast majority of the time is that a hydrogen atom and an oxygen atom come together to preserve its own unique form. So as the incoming electron changes its valence, changes its gravitational field, all this sort of thing, it pushes it off. The other choice that this atom has is to relax, let go and let this incoming electron change its whole life. And, when it does, it becomes water. Now, that changes everything. It goes to a much higher level of organization. A molecule of water is a much more complicated entity than an atom of hydrogen.

I believe the same thing is true with traders. When new information comes in, we make a choice. We can stick with our old belief systems, or we can let go and be open and let chaos organize a new and totally different belief system at a higher level. And going back to these five levels of trader development, I think that's the way you go from one level to the other. It's not by pushing, but by staying on a plateau and just being open to new possibilities. And in time you will automatically move up. Chaos, unfortunately, is a bad term. Chaos really is a dynamic form of order.

Q: And what, then, is intuition from this perspective?

Bill: Intuition is allowing this incoming information to come in and allowing it to reorganize your perspective or belief system or whatever. And that's why, when we talk about women's intuition, men—most of us—don't understand it. I believe it's because their level of organization is very different from ours.

Q: So, to put it very simply, Bill, intuition from this perspective is to be open to learn new things, whether it's from the market or from yourself. Is that it?

Bill: Absolutely. It's an openness and receptivity to new information. For example, today the bonds went lower than I think most people thought they were going to. I'm sure that brokers all over the world were calling around and saying, "Hey, what's going on? Why are the bonds down so much?" And from our standpoint, the bonds are going down for one reason: because they're going down. You see, the market is exactly where it's supposed to be. All the reasons that you will read about—it was a short-covering rally and they're waiting for the announcement next Friday, and this sort of thing—are basically baloney. I mean, the guys who write this stuff are paid to say something; they're not paid on the basis of the truthfulness of their statements.

Q: Bill, from your viewpoint, are there different kinds of intuition?

Bill: I think there are different applications of intuition. And I certainly think there are all sorts of levels of intuition. But I think intuition is very, very simple. I think intuition is just being in some kind of harmony with everything that is going on around you.

Q: I think of it as just being in a relaxed state of mind and body that allows you to make new information available to yourself. In fact, lots of time when we get an intuition, as you know, it often comes to us in a way that seems totally off the wall and out of the blue.

Bill: I couldn't agree with you more. One of the benchmarks that we look at very carefully is that anytime that you are not allowing information to come in, you tense your physical muscles.

And consequently, to be effective at trading, it's very important not to allow yourself to get tense. You must stay focused and relaxed.

Again, I don't give a hoot which way the market's going. If I want the market to go one way or the other, then I'm getting in my own way. But it is important to know which way "we're going," and so we monitor ourselves in terms of physical and psychological tension very carefully. I have yet to see a losing trader where his trading does not have some consequence to it, who does not tense up physically.

Q: Bill, in your opinion, how do successful traders tap into their intuition? How do they learn to trust it in order to operate more effectively on a consistent basis in the market?

Bill: I think that one of the words you just said is the key, and that's trust, having faith; like when we all have ultimate faith that the sun is coming up tomorrow. We don't know it for sure, but we have ultimate faith that it is. And a young child doesn't know that, but she learns it very quickly. We're talking about trust and faith as in our faith in the universe. . . . Einstein once said that the most important question that you can ever ask is, "Is the universe a friendly place?"

I think the most important question any trader can ask is, "Is the market a friendly place?"

Q: You know, unsuccessful traders often represent the market as being a very hostile place. They'll talk about the market as being a poke in the eye or a wild animal, or they'll talk of it as being a money shredder, all sorts of negative metaphors and symbols.

Bill: Right. Threatening!

Q: Yes. Threatening. Threatening and destructive. I worked with one trader for a while who referred to the market as being carcinogenic!

Bill: I've had traders tell me it was a bear or gorilla or something life threatening too.

Q: I can vividly remember one trader I interviewed, who is a very well-known trader and highly successful, to illustrate how the opposite is true of his belief system. He truly believed that the only reason that the bell rang at 7:30 every morning at the exchange was to enrich him and his family.

Bill: Perfect.

Q: He really believed that!

Bill: I think that's absolutely essential. And anytime you feel antagonistic toward the market or fighting the market . . . and most traders feel like that . . . it's a dog-eat-dog market and the other dogs are all other traders. On the contrary, the really good traders that we've worked with and known are exactly the opposite. We've trained over 500 people now privately—for example, the executive vice president of the largest exchange in the world and head traders for a number of very large foreign banks. Some of these people really didn't need much training. But one of the things that we have noticed with all these traders— we're talking about the big traders who have made many millions of dollars trading in the market themselves from their own efforts—is that all of them have two basic characteristics. One is they have a great deal of self-confidence. But they're also very humble people. They're not show-offs; they're really, really nice, gentle people.

Whereas the other thing that we've noticed is that all of them have a deep feeling of gratitude. Not that they've made all this money, but that they live in a time that is exciting and have the opportunity to trade. I mean, they're just grateful that the market opens up in the morning and they can experience the fun of participating in it.

Q: That's very consistent with my experience as well. You mentioned the word "trust" before. Why is it so hard for most traders to trust their intuition or to recognize, even on a practical level, its importance to move them forward?

Bill: Well, I think the answer is very simple and very pervasive. I think it's our educational system. When you come up in the educational system, I think there's a big difference, for example, between solving problems and creating profits or creating something new. And in our culture we're not educated to trust our intuition. If you're in an English class or if you write something, you have to have footnotes or a bibliography that supports something that you say with somebody else's opinion.

In other cultures they put a great deal of emphasis and truth on intuition. And they use intuition to a remarkable degree as an enlightened way of knowing. We call it ESP and a lot of other things, but that's just to intellectualize it. So the more successful you are in our culture, for example, if you're a lawyer, you have to cite precedent cases and this sort of thing; all of that is anti-intuitive. So the more successful you are in most professions and occupations in our culture, the more difficult it is for you to become a successful trader.

Q: Can you think of a specific example of a trader whose intuition you helped develop? And how did you do it?

Bill: Well, yes. As a matter of fact, I just received a fax from a person who was here quite some time ago and came back again to visit us a couple of months ago. This person is a Korean living in Korea. He was ten years old when the Korean conflict was going on. He was an orphan, no parents. His parents were killed.

He was adopted off a garbage truck by a sergeant in

the army. And although he's Korean, he has an Irish name. And he became a highly successful and well-known commercial artist in New York City. Then he decided to go into business and went into the import-export business, selling mostly to the Arabs. And from that, he went into real estate in California. From that, he went into trading. His first experiences with trading were very difficult. They were totally nonsuccessful. But I should add, now he is trading very well. And the fax we received said that what made the difference for him was he got back in touch with the artist inside himself.

Q: That's very interesting!

Bill: And you see he is now trading as an artist rather than as a businessman.

Q: Well, I think that supports my idea that traders who are getting good results in the market very often are operating on almost an artistic or aesthetic level.

Bill: Oh, I believe that completely!

Q: Do you believe that there are specific exercises one can do for enhancing intuition?

Bill: Yes, I do.

Q: Could you relate a few, because I know you have studied and have had considerable experience and involvement with the mind-body relationship as it relates to trading.

Bill: There is a book by Julia Cameron, entitled *The Artist Way*. We incorporate some of her work in our tutorials and our training sessions. She has devoted much of her career to working with other artists whose creativity has been blocked for some reason. Speaking of creativity, that is why I think her work applies to traders as well.

If you're not making a profit, then you're not in tune with the market and your creativity is, at least in some respects, blocked. Her approach is very, very simple— our family has been doing it, everybody who works here does it regularly. The first thing you do before you do anything else in the morning, before you eat breakfast or do anything else except possibly visit the bathroom, is sit down and write three pages. Now, it doesn't matter what you write. It's just pure stream of consciousness. If you're thinking, God, I don't know what I'm going to write, you write down, God, I don't know what I'm going to write. You do this every day, seven days a week, without any exceptions.

What it seems to do is drain the left hemisphere. It gets rid of all the chit-chat that goes on in our minds.

Q: It's like taking a mental enema, right?

Bill: Exactly! A good description. And it becomes fun! You will be surprised at the insights that come up. It allows intuition to start surfacing. Plus it does it first thing in the morning. So then you go to your trading or whatever, and you go with a free brain!

Then the second part is that you go out on the weekends or some time during the week and you have a date with yourself. Now, we have sort of bastardized this, and we call it the inner trader, the big IT. And you do something by yourself, you don't let anybody go with you, don't let anybody horn in. You do whatever by yourself. You go to a toy store and buy a slinky and play with it if you want to. Or you go to a movie or you take a long walk by yourself. The point of all this is that every morning you're giving up part of your left brain. And then on the weekends, with your date with your IT, you're receiving and acknowledging your right brain! I read somewhere that Einstein used to wonder why all of his good ideas came to him in the shower. They didn't come to him while he was sitting at his desk or in his office. And I think the same thing is true here. Interestingly, my own personal trading took a huge leap forward the first day I started this regimen. Now, it could be coincidence; it could be causative. I don't care. I mean, it doesn't matter. The fact is that it happened! Almost every day we get reports from people about how much this routine has helped their trading and improved their enjoyment of trading, which as you have written, is equally important.

Q: So I guess what we're getting from all this is that intuition is very closely aligned to a positive state of mind, which correlates well with your concept that trading at the highest level is a pure state-of-mind experience.

Bill: Well said!

Q: I think the analogy that works best for me is athletics, and it is consistent with the idea of "flow" that we were speaking about before. When athletes are relaxed, only then can they be truly confident, embrace a friendly universe, an internal universe of unlimited possibility, if you will. With this state of mind they're almost destined to have a successful result, providing, of course, that they have mechanical or technical competence, personal enthusiasm, and passion for that activity.

Bill: I think you're right. And I think there's another criterion too that parallels that and maybe even underlies it, and that is the whole concept that we mentioned earlier of honesty with yourself. That if you can get to the point where you're not lying to yourself, then that openness unlocks the door for intuition. But if you're lying to yourself, it seems to slam that door shut!

Q: Well, you know what I find? It's very tough for most traders. Particularly at the novice level, because they manufacture all kinds of apocryphal reasons to rationalize what they are doing wrong.

Bill: Right.

Q: You know, it's clear that they are wrong, but the excuses keep coming. I'm really not wrong, it's . . . fill in the blank!

Bill: That's exactly what I'm talking about . . . lying.

Q: I noticed that in his book *Zen and the Markets* (Warner, 1992), Ed Toppel has a very simple exercise. He offers three numbers: 27, 28, and 29. The question he asks is, Which is the greatest and which is the smallest? Then he says, if you can determine the answer, only then are you ready to trade.

Bill: Right. I agree with that. I like that book.

Q: Then why do you think most people find such difficulty in being honest with themselves?

Bill: I think it goes back to our discussion about chaos. Now, obviously, I am really prejudiced toward the science of chaos, and I see things in that term. That's sort of my paradigm. But let's say, for example, that you're a youngster and that you have a mother who is not overly friendly to you. And she comes on to you as an authoritarian figure and sort of scares you a bit and you're afraid of her and you're afraid of her criticism. And so you develop a whole strategy of subtle tactics to deal with this overpowering and menacing figure.

Now what happens when you develop this strategy? It becomes a strategy of resistance against information. That's organization. That's antichaos, antiacceptance of chaos! So then you encapsulate this. It becomes habituated in you and you don't notice it. So you grow up thinking that people don't like you, and you take this unconsciously with you to the market or wherever. Let's say that you come into your office in the morning and something is going on and everybody in your office is busy. So they're not paying attention to you. But you're coming in and your belief system is that nobody really likes you all that much. Because they don't jump up and say, Hi, Bob, how are you doing? You say, Yep. That's right. I knew it. Nobody likes me! Now you become aloof. And you don't communicate with them. And all these attitudes and actions have consequences. Then what they do is they say, Bob's kind of aloof. You know, he doesn't like us either. So what we have is what we call the bar syndrome, B-A-R. You have a belief. And that belief causes certain actions. And those actions cause reactions by other people to reinforce your belief.

This same phenomenon applies to losing traders.

Q: What I always say to traders when I work with them is consider the possibility that what you believe about yourself might not necessarily be an accurate representation of reality.

Bill: Yes. And it's very difficult because it's usually never questioned.

Q: Exactly. Bill, in your opinion how does the whole issue of intuition relate to market indicators?

Bill: Well, what we have found is that there's no intuitive indicator. We have found that what helps us most in the market is basically momentum indicators based on the science of chaos. And we follow very, very few indicators! Basically what we look at is what we call a balance line in chaotic terms between two strange attractors—one that's pulling prices up and one that's pulling them down. We look at a unique kind of momentum indicator that we have. And we look at the volume. That's all we look at. We can look at any market on any time frame, analyze the entire chart, and know exactly what we should be doing on each bar in ten seconds or less. I think that it's crucially important to be able to get in touch with the market in an instant. What most traders that we've worked with do is get latched on to the market. The monitors are the electronic drug. And it's very addicting. And they go a short in the bonds and then they can't see anything else except the bonds. And they overlook the opportunities that are in other places. So I think from an intuitive standpoint that what you were saying before about people's belief systems has to be at the base of all this, a basic trust of the market.

The concept of a market has been going on for at least five thousand years. It's probably going to go on as long as there are people around who have a difference of opinion about price and value. There are people out there who have made money consistently over long periods of time.

The market is neutral. The market doesn't care whether I am a millionaire or go bankrupt today.

The feeling of trust, of oneness with the market, is like getting to know a dog. If you have a very ferocious dog, the first time you see it you might be scared to death. But as you get to know it better and know its habits and get close to it and it gets close to you, there's no fear. Same thing happens with the market.

Q: I like to think of the market more as a cuddly puppy.

Bill: Yes. Very few people do, though. Most people think of it as something much more threatening than that.

Q: Well, thank you very much, Bill. Is there anything else about intuition that you feel we have not taken into consideration?

Bill: I can't think of anything. I want to be sure, though, and tell you that this is an important book. We have a flood of books on the market about technical indicators. We also have advertisements everywhere that say, use my mechanical systems, that will make the difference. We are told, take yourself out of the market. I think that advice is exactly wrong, exactly the wrong path to follow.

I think developing your intuition, becoming open to the information of the market will always be key to trading.

Q: It's a lot easier, as you know, to give traders more reasons to develop left-brain categories. It's a bit more subtle and probably more honest to get them to realize that successful trading is all about learning more about yourself.

Chapter Four

Richard McCall, Ph.D.

*Dr. Richard McCall is the founder and director of the Zen-Mind™ Challenge for Trading Professionals, and the president of Zen-Mind™ International, Inc. He holds a doctorate in Occupational Psychology and has studied and taught applied Zen for over thirty-five years to students throughout the world. He also holds advanced black belt rankings in Japanese kendo, karate and ninjutsu, and was a 1986 inductee in the International Martial Arts Hall of Fame. Dr. McCall is the author and pro-*ducer of "ZEN And The Art Of Financial Risk-Taking" (*Zen-Mind Publications, 1994*) and "The WAY Of The Warrior-Trader: The Financial Risk-Taker's Guide To Samurai Courage, Confidence and Discipline" (*Irwin Professional Publishing, 1996*). He now works exclu-*sively teaching applied Zen and peak-performance psychology to trading professionals.*

Q: Richard, could you begin by telling me something about yourself and how you became interested in trading?

Richard: My background and training are in the martial disciplines. My family lived in Japan when I was a child. My father is a lifetime Air Force officer, and I was raised around Japanese culture. I practiced a variety of martial arts disciplines, including Kendo and Kenjutsu.

When I returned to the States my teachers encouraged me to pursue everything related to the mind and personal development. That is how I developed a long history of working both in martial arts disciplines and in the field of psychology.

I started in the martial arts when I was six. I've been doing this for some time now. After high school I pursued an education in the field of psychology, particularly applied and occupational psychology.

Q: When did it occur to you that there was a serious link between psychology and trading? How did you put the two together?

Richard: At first, I didn't consider the trading aspect of it. It was brought to my attention by a handful of traders in the Little Rock area. I was teaching a martial arts class when a group of traders related to me that they had been reading the book *The Art of War* and began to see a real parallel between trading and the martial arts disciplines. In fact, the way they worded it was that trading was true warfare! As they related it to me, the difference was that the warfare of trading occurred between their ears.

So, they thought it would be worthwhile to investigate anything in the way of warrior discipline that might be to their advantage as traders—whether martial arts or Zen might be of a practical use to them.

After I developed some sense of what trading was all about, it became clear to me that there was a strong parallel between warriorship and trading, that the pursuit of the disciplines practiced by the martial artists of Japan would be to their advantage as traders.

Q: Richard, could you say something about some of the central concepts of Zen and the other Japanese martial arts disciplines for our readers who might not be familiar with them?

Richard: I appreciate the opportunity to do just that. First, let me address the issue of Zen. Zen in the United States is widely misunderstood as being a religion. In fact, its origin is religious, deriving from Buddhism. However, as it's practiced today, Zen is no longer a religion, but rather a psychological discipline. Zen itself is very nondescript. I will, however, try to give examples of what Zen is, because most individuals in fact have had a Zen-like experience.

Zen is basically a philosophy of awareness, its purpose being to make an individual more aware of his environment, of the things that go on around him and within him as well. Zen makes people aware of what we call their center: the center of their body, the center of their thoughts, and the center of their emotions.

So, one of the precepts of Zen is just that, to define and maintain one's center. Now, Zen also expands out to many other things. It has cultivated an appreciation, one might even say a celebration, of the moment, which is a very interesting psychology in contrast to the Western point of view where we are always looking ahead. We focus on forecasting. We do a lot of planning. Of course, these things are necessary. But Zen enables the individual to come back into the moment in the fullest possible way. There are many Zen stories along these lines. The individual in the story is suddenly and sometimes shockingly made aware of the moment. And in that moment, he's in a state of total bliss. And as I mentioned, the central precept of the practice of Zen is staying in the moment, fully aware, fully alive, and fully cognizant of one's existence. You can readily see why it is a compelling psychological discipline. Of course, Zen today is most well known through books that focus on the Samurai. The Samurai I've always considered to be an excellent role model or example of what human potential really can be. Now it's not to say that I would endorse all their politics or their particular way of life. But I do certainly respect what the Samurai were able to accomplish through their arts and disciplines. As you know, they had no choice. They were born right into a risk-taking, life-threatening profession. And in order to survive facing almost certain death on any given day, they had to develop a very strong sense of moral structure and a sense of discipline and ethics. And what evolved through the centuries was a code, a living code of behavior known as Bushido. The word "Bushido" is comprised of three words. The word *Bu* itself is "war." *Shi* means "man." And *Do* means "way." It translates as "The way of the warrior."

And so the Bushido code came to be a set of tenets or rules that the Samurai would live and die by. There was nothing more powerful or more important to them than adhering to their code. Everything revolved around Bushido. One of the advantages in modern times is that man, particularly in the Western world, tries to live by a set of ethics that are somewhat nondescript. The Bushido code, in contrast, is very descript and nails down exactly how an individual should live. At the core was Zen, which gave the Samurai the opportunity to maintain a sense of an emotional, spiritual, and physical center. I should remind you that this all served a very practical purpose. It enabled them to be truly formidable warriors who could face their own demise at any given instant in time and still maintain consistent performance and a high sense of intuition, that is, intuition about what the opponent might do or the direction the battle might take.

Q: Richard, in a description of your training program, "Zen and the Art of Financial Risk Taking," you write, "Zen and the Art of Financial Risk Taking will arm your trader's psyche with the timeless wisdom, insights and secrets of history's most accomplished professional risk taker, the legendary Samurai." Do you really feel trading is like fighting on a battlefield where one is engaged in a life and death struggle?

Richard: I believe that's absolutely true. The markets are unmerciful. They will continue to act and react whether or not you are ready for them. As people enter the market and prepare to invest their money, to assume risk, they must be prepared for battle. They have to be on their fullest possible guard, to be at their fullest possible level of alertness. We call this peak performance readiness. The only way that I know to do this on an effective, ongoing basis is through martial disciplines.

Now, obviously, there are other ways to approach this psychology. And I have read many books that I know your readers will be familiar with that speak of the preparation necessary before entering the markets. I think, though, that if you dissect the recommendations that are given, you will find Zen-like advice at the core.

Q: From your perspective, Richard, could you identify a formula for success in trading?

Richard: Yes. Consistent profitable trading depends on three things: adequate financing, patience, and emotional-behavioral discipline.

Q: And that's where Zen and the art of financial risk taking can help?

Richard: Absolutely! The first and foremost thing, of course, is financing. I mean, if you're going to enter into an economic war or a financial war, you need the money to back up your endeavor. I think that goes without saying.

The second thing, as I mentioned, is patience. It doesn't matter what type of financial risk an individual is undertaking, whether in the real estate markets, the stock markets, or the futures markets. There has to be an element of patience involved. In other words, you're entering a position and you need the patience to see what this position will do. Hopefully, it will go in the chosen direction. But it may not. And it takes patience. And the warriors certainly understood this, that they could not be "flinchy" in the face of their opponents' motions. Patience is probably the single most important psychological attribute a person can have in undertaking financial risk. Of course, along with this, a person has to exercise behavioral discipline and consistency.

The appropriate metaphor here would be the use of the sword for the Samurai. The Samurai had to be able to engage the opponent and use *his* school or *his* technique. And I like to use the parallel of a trading system. Every swordsman had a style or a system of swordplay that he employed. And he had to be able to employ this style again and again with absolute precision and flawless consistency.

So, I think those three things are critical to trading success. You have to have, first, the money to trade; second, the patience; and third, the consistency to execute with absolutely flawless precision.

Q: Richard, let's talk patience for a moment. In my experience, I think very often traders confuse patience with an inability to act. I say this because traders will wait a long time for something to materialize, and just at the moment when action is required, they find themselves unable to act with certainty. How do you understand the concept of patience from your particular vantage point? And how does that understanding enhance the likely performance of the trader who studies with you?

Richard: Well, I think it's important to understand that patience is the reflection of a philosophy. Zen philosophy teaches that the universe moves in cycles. Everything has its time. That's one of the universal laws in the martial arts disciplines. It is referred to as "the grand truth."

Q: Kind of like Ecclesiastes, everything has its season.

Richard: Exactly! And in the case of trading, the market is cyclical. You know that the economy is going to ebb and flow. And every investor is trying to simply catch that wave. If you recognize the fact that you cannot have an economy, you cannot have a market without that ebb and flow, then you begin to realize that patience is actually required in order to make money. In other words, you must wait for the cycles in order for you to be able to take the profit out of the market.

As I look at patience, I see that it's just like fighting an opponent with a sword. And the practice of Kendo, our modern version of Samurai sword fighting, always waits for the opponent to either lower his blade or raise it up. We can't attack with the blade straight in our face. And so patience, according to our philosophy, is just common sense when you really get down to it. There needs to be ebb and flow for you to enter and get what you need from the market or from your opponent. So the way I look at patience is understanding that essential truth.

I want to comment on developing emotional and behavioral discipline. If you're going to play the markets, you must have a life philosophy that accepts wholly and completely that there are cycles and that cycles are an absolute necessity. Going back to the issue of behavioral discipline as it relates to this, in the martial arts there are two things we seek to eliminate. This applies directly to trading. Those two things are ego and flinching. The ego is a subject widely discussed in trading; it's discussed from several angles. But the way we look at ego is that ego is that component in us that says we are right when we are not necessarily correct! We think we know what the opponent is going to do, we think we know what the market is going to do despite the fact that we are obviously wrong. We have to eliminate the ego, and in turn, we also have to eliminate the flinch reflex which is so normal and so common in humankind. Things happen and then we get a knee-jerk reaction to it. That's when patience leaves you. Because if something happens and we flinch, we don't hold our ground and we don't maintain our patience.

Q: Can you talk more specifically about the two phenomena as they relate to trading? How do *you* teach someone to subdue their ego or eliminate it? And then we can talk a little bit about flinching, because I think as people are reading this interview, they're thinking about the many times that they've had to flinch in the market and with what consequences.

Richard: You have to remember that the Samurai did not go into the battle unprepared. It was the daily practice of emotional control through Zen that gave them the kind of control on an instinctive level that they needed when they were in the battle. They had been training and preparing themselves for endless hours for that one moment when they would engage the opponent.

          So going back now to the issue of how do you prepare yourself, the trader really needs to approach training himself from a fresh point of view. Most traders have a tendency to think of preparation as intellectual or academic in nature. They like to "study" the markets, to judge the economics of a particular market. They forget, in the final analysis, that the bottom line of trading is that it is up to their mind and their emotions and their control to take action when the time is right!

And so traders have to condition and prepare themselves. One way to condition yourself is to repeatedly play the markets. In other words, you get used to the idea through trial and error. But there are other ways as well. The practice of Zen employs a meditative technique referred to as zazen, which means seated meditation.

Q: Seated meditation?

Richard: Yes. Za Zen teaches an individual to control his mind in that particular moment. As he sits practicing this meditation, the objective of the meditation is to have no thought at all. Ironically, most people meditate thinking about something. The objective of zazen is to think of nothing, which is probably the most difficult task that you can undertake—to clear the mind of any thought, transient or otherwise, for a period of time. With daily practice of this discipline, you learn to control the thoughts that cross your mind. This is an important training for traders, because the thoughts that cross your mind cause you to flinch.

The Samurai would enter into a state of mind in which their minds were empty, where they couldn't flinch. This state of mind is called Mushin. When they achieved the state of Mushin, then and only then did they function without flinching and without ego entering the picture.

The objective of Zen teaching is to teach the individual how to empty the mind to prepare for whatever is in front of him in order to flow without encumbrance. That's the goal. Now, there are many other things about Zen that add to this overall training; however, the primary objective is still to teach you the discipline of controlling your mind and its receptivity to the truth as it unfolds in front of you.

Q: Richard, could you give me a sense of what your daily regimen is like? How you personally prepare on a day-to-day basis for trading?

Richard: At this time, even though my trading is part-time, I approach each day with the intent of training my body and spirit: I practice as much exercise as possible. I'll run two or three miles in the morning. At that point, while resting or cooling down from the run, I like to medidate using zazen, which I mentioned earlier, to clear my mind of any distractions. After that, I like to focus my mind by intentionally deciding whether or not I will be trading. At this point I make a cognitive decision whether I'm going to be a warrior on the financial front or not. I try to engage the market three days a week. My current interest is the S&P 500. My trading is expanding gradually with the passing of time. However, I make it a point to practice as much financial risk taking as I can.

And with a smile on my face, I'd like to mention that long before learning about trading, I had seen the parallel of playing blackjack in the casinos we have near us in Little Rock. And on a routine basis, at least once a week, I try to practice financial risk taking and emotional control in that arena, because it's on a smaller scale and it tends to move faster.

Q: Sounds good! I have to try that one on my wife. A little blackjack to improve my mental reflexes!

Richard: It's a good way to practice.

Q: It's a good way to get into the casino.

Richard: Casino gambling is really a great way to practice your control because it's a faster pace. And, in my opinion, it is a parallel to the way the markets move up and down. You can see the trends forming very quickly. Then you practice your control with those trends: either staying in or exiting the game.

Q: Richard, you have spoken before about the importance of optimism and hopefulness and the ability to exhibit those attitudes in your trading. Can you talk a little bit about that because, from my perspective, this is key.

Richard: That's an interesting question. I am a firm believer in the power of positive thinking.

    I've met all types of traders. And the ones I work with usually are currently having a difficult time of it. Otherwise, they wouldn't have consulted with me. I have been surprised at the number of traders who enter the market with a pessimistic or negative attitude, in other words, they are anticipating their loss before they get in there. Interestingly, they are able to create this self-fulfilling prophecy.

    On the other hand, there are traders who say, I'm going into the market and I'm going to win, I'm going to reap a profit from this trade. And surely it's true that they're not going to reap a profit every time, but since thinking is an ongoing process, it may as well be a positive thinking process. The point is, it's strictly to their advantage.

Q: Well, as you know, Richard, I've written quite a bit on this particular subject. My feeling is very strong on this point. If one enters a trade with the attitude that "they're out to get me," that's exactly what's going to happen! That's not to say that if one is positive, each trade is going to be successful. But I know one thing for sure: if you approach the whole process with an attitude of optimism, the results will be far better in the long run.

Richard: Oh, definitely better in the long run. I believe one of the great shortcomings of traders is that they reduce the whole trading process into independent trades. They tend to live and die on each trade rather than viewing the whole process of trading as just that, a process.

    That reminds me of our conversation about the differences between Eastern and Western traders. I've observed that the traders in the Far East tend to view trading as a process, in fact as an art form, rather than as a way to make money in a particular position.

    They tend to see the challenge of the trade rather than the benefit of the profit. And I have seen that approach to be much more successful in the long run, because they approach the game as just that. It's a game rather than a way to make money today!

Q: It's interesting that you mentioned that, because many of the traders whom I've interviewed, although they did not refer to trading as an art form per se, have reported that they were trading for the inherent enjoyment and personal satisfaction of doing well, not for the profit motive.

Richard: I think that brings us to a very important issue: passion. Passion and the love of what you do is where the true Zen of that behavior comes in. And it reminds me of the passion exhibited in the traditional Japanese arts, whether it is bonsai tree growing or the tea ceremony or archery. You don't engage in these disciplines for the sake of creating another miniature tree or brewing a tasty cup of tea or shooting an arrow to hit a target. You do it for the sensation of the wholeness of the experience.

That's why I say traders whom I have known to be very successful are totally involved in the process of intuitively reading what's going on in the market and responding in a way that allows them to create themselves. It is their passion that assures their success.

Q: Well, I'm glad you mentioned the concept of intuition, because, as you know, this book is about intuition. From your perspective, what exactly is intuition?

Richard: I have observed that there are basically two kinds of intuition. And let me add, this observation is endorsed by the Japanese masters I work with as well. First, there is a sensory intuition, and I'll give a definition of it in just a minute. And, second, there is a supersensory intuition. One leads to the other. First the sensory. It is an impression that an individual gets at the preconscious level, a cumulative insight of all the bits of data and information that the mind is storing and gathering and coordinating. When it finally comes out to be a feeling, that is the intuition. Remember, it is a feeling that's based on some sort of internal processing of information. Again, it's at the preconscious level. It's been my observation that this particular feeling emanates from the right brain. We talk often in psychology about left-brain and right-brain functions.

Q: It's very interesting that you're mentioning this, because it's been my experience that trading successfully at the highest level is almost entirely a right-brain activity.

Richard: I agree with that 100 percent. And when we learn a skill, obviously we employ our left brain to learn and acquire the skill. But when we begin to engage our skill and to use it precisely, the right brain kicks in. That's how we become automatic or intuitive traders.

Q: Bill was saying that our left brain has two primary functions.

Richard: Exactly true. So again my observation is that there is a sensory intuition that is the combination of all our sensory inputs accumulating in our mind at the preconscious level until we finally get a feeling. But then as this intuitive skill advances, one has more Zen-like experiences in trading and everything else.

Q: You mean being in that moment or having a full appreciation of the richness and texture of the experience?

Richard: Exactly. They have become one with their experience. In other words . . .

Q: One with the market?

Richard: Yes, with the trading experience. At that particular point, intuition can graduate. It can graduate up to the extrasensory level. Because I have seen and heard many a case and heard many a story about individuals who began to sense what the market was doing even though they were not monitoring the market in the conventional sense.

Q: Richard, are you saying that they get so in tune with the unfolding of the market that they can actually unconsciously feel what the market will do next? In other words, they can tap into the next logical unfolding of the market?

Richard: I believe that to be true. Those are my two observations about intuition. And, by the way, I believe both levels of intuition are learnable.

It is important to remember that people must go through a patient series of learning experiences before intuition develops. But it does develop, and it must be the by-product of acquiring more and more information and then letting go.

Q: Richard, I think this is very interesting because, from my point of view, intuition is making oneself available to learn new things. In other words, that you are opening yourself to experience what the market will do next. Is that consistent with your understanding?

Richard: It is, and it isn't.

Q: Can you be more specific?

Richard: Sure. What I think is more important than making yourself available to the information is having a prearranged or a preconceived response.

If we employ the analogy of the mind being a computer, we know that an empty disk is open to receive information. We also know that a programmed disk is ready to respond to what we put in. That's why we want to be sure to program the disk of the mind, that is, condition it on a routine, daily basis to be ready to respond to whatever is confronting it in terms of new information.

Q: And intuition allows you to respond to that program?

Richard: Absolutely. And most importantly, it allows you to respond to it as quickly and as efficiently as possible.

Q: Now, do you think successful traders are tapping into their intuition in ways that are different from the way most people do?

Richard: Unquestionably, yes. When I look at martial arts disciplines, I see people who go through years of training in just one technique. I see them go through the dedication, commitment, and sacrifice of learning and relearning these techniques. A better word would be learning and refining these techniques. The good martial artist is one whose eyes become almost blank when faced with the opponent. What you are looking at is an individual moving into the state of Mushin or empty mind, which is again the ultimate objective of Zen. Successful traders do the same thing. I've seen those who I think are successful traders, and I've seen those who I think are less successful. The ones who are successful watch their screens with a sense of open-minded, nonjudgmental clarity.

Q: So, a very practical application of this idea might be somebody who has a system that is as simple as support and resistance. If he really believes in the system and has tested it out to be true over time, then what he would have to do is execute without second-guessing himself. He would just really have to believe in the system. And if he was proven wrong, then he would just take the next appropriate action: get out with a small loss.

Richard: Exactly. And nothing could get the Samurai killed quicker than to second-guess his system of engagement. Nothing. It's true with trading as well. You cannot go into trade and try to change systems in the midst of the battle. Nothing could be more deadly or more quickly spell disaster for the trader.

Q: Richard, in your experience, why do you believe it's so hard for most traders to trust their intuition?

Richard: Fear. I mean, fear is a very strong motivator. I don't believe that there is a trader anywhere who doesn't practice his system on paper before employing it in the market. And I think that most traders have proven to themselves it can work. But I've seen enough examples, not only in trading, where people have this attitude of what we call sequential verifiability for failure. They begin to see that "this" just burned me and, therefore, I have validation for my fear. The fact is that what they don't have to offset their fear is a philosophy and a recognition that the markets are cyclical—that you have to take losses in order to take profits, that you must have patience and maintain emotional and psychological balance. They tend to hold onto the memory of the fact that they just had one or two or three sequential hits where they took losses. They hold onto a validation of their belief to continue the cycle of fear.

Q: Richard, you were saying before that you believe that intuition is something that's learnable. Can you be more specific?

Richard: We have a number of drills that we employ to help people develop intuition. When the mind is open and clear, as I've described earlier, then they're able to be more intuitive. It's amazing, if you do something as simple as play with balloons, it sounds funny, a child's game.

Q: I saw one of the items on your program is balloons and bricks. Is that the exercise?

Richard: Yes. I get an individual to inflate three 13-inch balloons and then tap them in a room that has a ceiling high enough to do it. Just tap the balloon into the air and then throw the second balloon into the air. And then doing so, they're just concentrating on keeping two balloons in the air simultaneously. Now this allows the brain to shift back and forth from one balloon to the other. But if you add a third balloon as you would in juggling, for example, you throw the third balloon in, and the third balloon enters and creates an element of conflict, an element of unpredictability. And so what we do at our Dojo is teach people "silly" little games like this. And I say silly in quotation marks because they're really very potent kinds of experiences. Keeping the three balloons airborne will clear the mind enough for a person to open up to his intuitive impulses. Before you know it, he can actually sense where the balloon is about to move. So, using that as a metaphor for the market, I have been experimenting and researching with traders, asking them to do drills of this type. Particularly in my home training program. Do this exercise on a daily basis as an experiment and have fun for a period of, say, six months.

Q: I imagine one of the things that comes out of this exercise is that the trader stops thinking about the balloons. He just really has to go after those balloons.

Richard: Good. That's exactly the objective. It is no longer to pursue the balloons with your mind, but to let go to the experience and keep the balloons aloft.

It's important to remember, too, going back to the issue of preparing yourself for intuition, that traders unquestionably tend to overintellectualize trading. In doing so, the more intellectual your approach, the less you are able to be intuitive and responsive in the moment.

Q: I think that's right on target. What I always say in my seminars is that trading has very little to do with knowing and everything to do with doing. And the closer you can get to the "do," the more you will know.

Richard: Exactly.

Many of the people who have gone to our Zen-Mind™ Challenge comment on the importance of following a ritual. When you walk into the facility, there is a certain etiquette to be followed. You have to bow toward the center of the room. When you exit, you must do the same thing. You can't walk in with your shoes on. The point is that the following of the ritual seemed to lead to a behavioral discipline within.

It's been my observation with traders that ritual really is of great significance. Traders develop rituals as all high-level performing athletes do. When a baseball player comes up to bat, he may tap his right shoe and then his left shoe and then roll the bat around 360 degrees in his hand. Ritual is important, because ritual allows you to maintain consistency and grow. And, again, a ritual is behavioral discipline.

Q: And the consistency, where does that come in?

Richard: The consistency is that you can't allow yourself to ever do anything that will not enhance your trading behavior, and you just do not allow yourself to ever do that behavior without ritual. So this doesn't sound too esoteric, let me give you an example. Before calling in an order, many of the traders will go through a ritual that they engage in. They have a hesitancy about placing orders. So I'll have them engage in ritual before they place the order. When they see their indicators come up, they will go ahead and execute the ritual. It can be something as simple as drawing a picture on a piece of paper. It can be a quick scribble. It can be a hand motion. But the ritual leads them, through conditioning, to follow their prescribed behavior, to execute their order or their signal, automatically.

Q: Basically, you are giving them an anchor, is that right?

Richard: Absolutely true.

Q: To help them cross the threshold into performing the activity.

Richard: Yes. I have them reinforce the behavior, both in the martial arts disciplines and in the markets. These are some of the things that I do to lead them to the next step of behavioral discipline.

Q: You know, it's interesting. One of the most successful floor traders on the Chicago Mercantile Exchange, one of the largest and consistently profitable traders, has a ritual that I believe bears mentioning. I interviewed him last year. After completing his trading card, as he puts it in his pocket, he always says, "Yeah."

Richard: Okay. That's exactly what I'm talking about.

Q: You know, he does this whether it's a winner or a loser. It's just to give him the motivation to go on strong to the next trade.

Richard: Exactly. It's a way for him to complete the process and then move on to the next one.

Q: And it's real interesting with this guy—by the way, his name is Donald Sliter. I asked him about that, and he said he developed this ritual because he sensed the feeling of letting down after he would have a loser. And he had to figure out some way within himself to be able to go on to the next trade with the same level of energy, resolve, and motivation that he would get from one good trade to the next good trade. He just came up with this thing on his own. And those of us who know this guy see him in action. He's a consistent money machine.

Richard: I respect and applaud anybody who can come up with that kind of ritual to solve his problem. As I mentioned earlier, everyone has had and continues to have various Zen-like experiences. And that's one of them.

Again, we can talk about neurolinguistic programming, or we can talk about Zen or about any number of behavioral strategies. They all contain many of the same basic components.

Q: How does discipline fit into your framework?

Richard: In the context of trading, I think the word discipline means one thing: executing your system flawlessly. I mean, that's the only true definition, and to execute a system with that kind of precision requires an incredible amount of discipline. That's why I say that people need to structure their lives; they need to structure their day-to-day existence around mind, body, and spirit disciplines. You see, it is not all that obvious that in order to end up with the behavioral discipline required to trade with profitability, you must have a code and philosophy.

Q: And the discipline from your perspective will also enhance their intuition about the markets?

Richard: That's where you make discipline your ritual! For example, I'm not a great fan of exercising, so I have to program myself to do it. I mean, I have the same agony when

I exercise as the next person. If I put my foot on the ground in the morning after getting out of bed, I can't rest based on my own preprogramming; I can't rest comfortably about my day unless I go outside and work out. I mean, rain or shine, it has to happen. You can call that an obsession or an obsessive-compulsive attitude. What it does is it guarantees that I'm going to start the day with this important component that I've determined is an internal element of existence. Commitment to excel!

Q: Richard, could you say something about the demonstration you gave at the Dow-Jones Telerate conference? I would like you to tell our readers about that incredible exercise and what its significance is.

Richard: I used that demonstration to make a point about risk taking. I had my wife, Lyndee, place a cucumber flush against the jugular vein of her neck. In doing this, she represented a target. She also represented what we call the inactive side of Zen. I then took a 42-inch-long Katana, Samurai sword. My objective—the mission, as we described it—was to make one cut completely through the cucumber, which was resting directly against the skin on her neck. Make one clean cut so that the cucumber becomes two pieces.

Q: And leave Lyndee in one piece?

Richard: Yes, Lyndee is always very emphatic about that! We simply set her up where she remains perfectly motionless. And my objective, again, is to make the blade cut the cucumber, using all the necessary precontrols that come from years of training and discipline.

Q: Do you do it intuitively?

Richard: It is not so much intuitive, but you can begin to sense that the person may flinch. Yes, intuition does enter the picture, but what you do is go into Mushin. And you clear the mind of anything that has happened to you prior to the demonstration and what may happen after the demonstration. The only thing that exists is the blade, the cucumber, and my hand. And so that's what we will call our kind of tunnel vision, self-created for the sake of peak performance, and obviously, it has to be consistent. Every single time it has to be consistent; otherwise, someone gets hurt. So that's the demonstration that we were doing. But it was to make a point. And that was, every day that we trade, every day that we enter into our risk endeavors, whatever they may be, we put our necks on the line. And our necks are figurative, in most cases, in the terms of our money.

In order to save our necks, in order to not get hurt, we have to have that kind of balance, of focus and consistency of behavior to be exactly precise to get what we need out of that situation. So in my demonstration I was describing what I call the Samurai action plan. The acronym is A-C-T-I-O-N. The first letter, "A," stands for accept all possible losses before entering the battle. Second letter, "C," stands for center yourself in mind, body, and spirit. The "T" stands for trust your inner skills and warrior intuition. "I" stands for imagine success clearly with your mind's eye. "O" stands for only exist in the present moment. And the final letter, "N," stands for never, never stop once you have begun. And if you take any situation or any behavioral objective that you may have, you will find that if you will follow that acronym, ACTION, you will be employing the collective mentality of the Samurai warrior.

Q: Richard, what would be your advice to someone who wants to move from being a mechanical trader to becoming an intuitive trader? What would you say are the preconditions that are necessary to make that change?

Richard: First, it would depend on where they are and how their life is structured. I think the first thing of importance here is, if you're talking purely superficial mechanical trading, the first thing of importance I would emphasize if I were going to create an intuitive trader is: trade full time. This is a must first off.

This is an important point because it addresses the issue of commitment. If they're going to commit fully and say, okay, I'm going to do this for X period of months or whatever, that's the first piece. The second piece is to recognize that much of trading really is only mechanical, in the sense that you have to use a precise system. You have to employ your chosen system, a system that you believe in. That system should have been tested, and you should have absolute faith in that system.

But I think the next piece of the puzzle to getting away from being such a mechanical trader is to develop the ability to let go. You have to let go in the heat of the battle and watch your system work. I really think that's a key word here in learning to let go. That, again, brings me back to my frame of reference, which is always the Japanese perspective. In Japan, the traders handle things differently. They are not so mechanistic. They will pay people to do their research and to do their forecasting. For them, trading comes right down to executing the trade. They just execute when the signals are there.

The fact is indisputable: when you really do trade well, you really cannot call it mechanical. You must be an intuitive trader!

Q: The trader I was telling you about earlier, Donald Sliter, conveyed to me that when he's trading, and these are his words, he's totally in a zone and he's unaware of himself or time or the literally thousands of contracts that he trades. In fact, he said to me when he comes home in the evening, he just feels his activity in the market was pure action. He has no sense of the distinction between himself and his trading. It's just pure and natural and effortless.

Richard: It sounds like a description of Zen. And when we train students, whether in the formal Dojo or in the seminars or retreats that I do, the best evaluation that a person can use to determine his progress is that whatever he is doing, whether it is clipping a bonsai tree or trading in the bean market, he begins to experience a sense of selflessness and timelessness. That, in fact, represents tremendous progress. Traders break through when their trading becomes raised to an art form rather than just a mechanistic way to make money.

Traders need to make a commitment to excel. It's very difficult to do anything of any high caliber without commitment. You can't trade half way. You must commit and prepare for trading. Financially prepare for it so that you know that you can live without any revenues or any profits being taken in from the market. But that would only be step number one. Step number two is look at yourself holistically. Don't try to approach trading just from an academic or scholarly point of view. It's not a matter of just knowing what the market is doing. It's being prepared to act on what the market is doing. I always encourage traders to work on themselves. And they really need to work on realizing that they trade only as well as they feel. It's essential to feel good, eat well, sleep well, rest well in order to be able to trade well. Those are the two most important things. The markets and your trading are a total reflection of your own personality. And they will surely show any weak links that exist.

Q: Let's talk for a moment about physiology. As you know, I believe the relationship between physiology and trading performance is highly correlated. It is always interesting to me that very few traders really give any significance to this. What is your point of view?

Richard: Let's imagine a triangle whose sides represent the body, the mind, and the spirit. We are all comprised of mind, body, and spirit. Now, we have talked a lot about spirit as it relates to Zen. But in reality the root of Zen is physiology, to get the body centered physically so the individual can perform flawlessly without internal hindrance. The best way to get the mind and the body to work together, day-to-day in a moment-by-moment basis, is breathing correctly. As a matter of fact, every mental discipline throughout the Far East and many of the Native American disciplines build their entire systems of discipline around breathing. Breathing is very important. If you notice that people are tense or if they are anxious or if they are not thinking well or not feeling well, you can nearly always find that there is a defect in the way that they breathe. In fact, it's interesting that the word for breathing is respiration. And the word itself goes back to the Greek, meaning renewal.

Q: We also have the word inspire.

Richard: Inspiration, that's right. Very true. Our lives are so connected to breathing that it's easy to overlook it. It's so simple.

People need to learn how to breathe. And that's why Yoga, or zazen, or the martial arts disciplines, or even exercise programs, for that matter, help enhance the person's psychological state. There's always an unquestionable relationship between one's state of mind and the physical state of the body. I encourage every single trader with whom I work to bring the mind-body spirits into balance and to practice breathing in order to maintain their center, to bring that triangle back into focus in their mind.

Q: If you think about the diet of the average trader on the trading desk, it's not exactly predictive of great performance results.

Richard: Exactly!

Q: Fries and cheeseburgers. I encourage my traders to take a very serious look at what they're shoveling into themselves.

Richard: It is so easy for traders to fall prey to that kind of low octane fuel coming into the body and then demanding really high octane performance of themselves. It doesn't make sense. We don't ask our vehicles to run like that.

Q: You said a moment ago that traders overlook the importance of breathing to their performance or their physiology because it's just so simple. It occurred to me that that's a pretty good generalization about trading, that people have a tendency to reject the obvious. There are so many aspects of trading that in a sense are really so blatant that traders reject them. If it's simple and obvious, I would argue, don't miss the point. That's the way it should be!

Richard: I agree 100 percent that the most important issues of our existence are usually right under our noses. I'm talking about the big stuff—health, happiness, and psychological well-being. All these things are so simple. They're always right in front of our face. And we consult specialists and gurus to find the answers. But most of these answers are right in front of us.

Q: It's ironic, isn't it, that when you climb a mountain to speak to a guru about the secret of life or consult a trading maven about the secret of trading, you're hoping for a complex answer.

It's unfortunate that there's a whole industry of individuals who represent themselves as gurus and keep promulgating the notion to the public that there's one objective answer to successful trading. Most of them have never personally achieved any success in the market at all.

Richard: I've been surprised by the relative complexity that has been built into trading psychology and trading efficiency. This reality strikes home sometimes with people who talk with me. When I say, this is what we can do to help improve your performance, their first impression usually is, that's it? And their second impression is, hey, that works!

I think the great traders realize it's right there in front of you. It's just a fact of life that if you do things in a natural and simple way and keep your mind clear and keep your body healthy, you will feel better. You will think better, and your mind will be more open and intuitive to the truth that evolves in front of you.

Q: You will be more open and intuitive because you have demonstrated the commitment. You have demonstrated strong conviction and determination to develop these qualities. You have put in the time and the effort that's required to take it to the next level so you are in a position where now you can be intuitive.

Richard: Of course, Zen is the obvious, what's really in front of you. What's real and what's honestly there. It's funny because after my demonstrations, I'll get comments from people who are listening to me, and they'll ask, When are you going to start talking about trading? The reality is, everything I'm doing comments on trading. They're simple, universal truths.

Q: They are trading, not about trading, right?

Richard: Absolutely true. So it always puts a smile on my face and certainly in my heart when I hear them looking for complexity and see them trying to find something more complex or this magic bullet.

Q: It reminds me of the comment of the monk to his disciple who is anxious to know what enlightenment is. The monk says, enlightenment is very simple. Before enlightenment there's chopping wood and carrying water. But after enlightenment there's chopping wood and carrying water.

Richard: That sums it up, doesn't it?

Chapter Five

Charles Faulkner

Charles Faulkner is a certified trainer and expert modeler of neurolinguistic programming (NLP), a technique designed to reproduce human excellence. He is coauthor of the Nightingale-Conant audiocassette program and book NLP: The New Technology of Achievement, *the audiocassette program "Success Mastery with NLP," and the videotape "NLP in Action." He was interviewed by Jack Schwager in* The New Market Wizards *(Harper Business, 1992) for his modeling of futures traders and by Howard Abell and me in* The Outer Game of Trading *(Irwin, 1994) on the topic of trading strategies.*

Q: Charles, I think it will be helpful to our readers, before I ask you about NLP's particular perspective on intuition, if you could explain exactly what NLP is?

Charles: NLP is short for neurolinguistic programming, though it might have been better named "natural learning processes." Quite simply, NLP is the study of human excellence—as it's found in real, live, living, breathing human beings. Only instead of just admiring success, NLP is a detailed discipline for discovering just how people do what they do so well, and then devising techniques for reproducing that excellence in others. It is probably best known through Anthony Robbins and other popular figures who use it to motivate and persuade, and through the books and lectures of John Bradshaw, who along with many therapists, use it to heal emotional wounds and change relationship difficulties. NLP particularly applies to our discussion of intuition, as NLP is much more than just a way of creating motivation and change, important as those are. NLP is fundamentally a model of how people think, act, and live. NLP modelers, such as myself, spend our time uncovering new models of human excellence, such as the structure of intuition.

Q: Charles, many people think of intuition as being able to look into the future or possessing some faculty like ESP. From your perspective, what is intuition?

Charles: In my view, intuition is simply getting a solution and not knowing how you got there. I know other people think of intuition as messages from the mother ship or channeling or something like that. Whether those things exist or not, they are not intuition as I know it. Intuition is when you get an insight into something that's a result from your experience with it.

Q: You know, Charles, traders are fascinated by the issue of intuition. However, the more I speak with traders about intuition, the more I have observed that, often, we are referring to vastly different experiences. According to your perspective, would a better understanding of intuition enhance trading performance?

Charles: Let's be clear about this. All our ideas start as intuitions. That is, we get an insight or an idea. Where did it come from? How do we know we can trust it? If it's important, then we take the time to consciously reason backwards, finding the logical inferences and creating the well-reasoned links that we know are trustworthy and will last through time. An idea turns into an algorithm, an insight into a system.

          This makes sense when you know that the brain is divided into different kinds of processing modules, among them the conscious and the unconscious. There is the old saw about the conscious mind being limited to seven plus or minus two. This was discovered by the great brain researcher Dr. George Miller. He found that human beings can consciously keep track of only about seven chunks of information at one time. It's one of the reasons that telephone numbers historically had seven digits. He also found the size of the chunk will vary with experience. When you are first learning a friend's new telephone number, it takes most of your conscious mind chunks available. With experience, this friend's number will become one chunk. This is true of everything we learn, whether it's driving, cooking, analyzing markets, or trading. On the other hand, and at the same time, your unconscious mind is processing millions of chunks of information, including your balance, breathing, vision, movement, understanding of language, speaking, and intuitions. This means we can put things together unconsciously that would overwhelm our conscious minds. The advantage of this is leaps of logic that often go to the heart of whatever the matter is. The disadvantage is that our insight into something may appear brilliant, but we don't know how we got there. We don't know if there are any faulty steps in our thinking process. Would a better understanding of this intuitive process enhance a trader's performance? It couldn't hurt, and it just might be crucial.

Q: Charles, are successful traders tapping into their intuition is a way that is different from what most traders are experiencing?

Charles: Yes, and not only in particular markets, but across their whole approach. This has been confirmed in "expert systems" research. When attempts were made to build an expert model of some skill (medicine, markets, law, etc.), it was found that one couldn't just take a novice and simply build up a large number of examples in him. AI (artificial intelligence) researchers found that real experts have a set of intuitions that are different from, and often contrary to, the kinds of insights or intuitions that novices will have. It turns out that the person who really becomes expert at something will, at some point, radically reorder his thinking and then arrive at insights that are quite different from the ordinary person's.

Q: Charles, I don't know if this is exactly the point that you
              are making, but this occurred to me as you were discuss-
              ing your view of intuition If someone sits down to the
              piano for the very first time and feels very intuitive about
              Beethoven's Emperor Concerto, I think you have to give
              it a little less credibility than in the case of the individual
              who has spent twenty years practicing and analyzing
              pieces and then feels a certain intuitive impulse about the
              meaning of the piece.

Charles: Yes, definitely. It's an educated inference. The novice
              trader is at a disadvantage because the intuitions that he
              is going to have about the market are going to be the ones
              that are typical of beginners. The expert is someone who
              sees beyond those typical responses and has an under-
              standing of the deeper workings of the market.

Q: So intuition from your point of view seems to be a form
              of creative thinking about something that you already
              know!

Charles: Exactly. Intuition does not come out of thin air. If it did,
              how would you know? I mean, suppose that you had a
              little voice in your head that said, "Wear your underwear
              on the outside." Now, truthfully, you might be a little
              concerned about paying attention to that voice, but Ma-
              donna did pay attention to that voice and it has really
              paid off! On the other hand, does she wake up in the
              morning with a feeling about the Swiss franc? The point
              is, even if she did, she wouldn't be in a position to act on
              it. (Well, financially yes, but as a seasoned trader with an
              intuition, no.) Trading is filled with stories of people who
              have taken years steeping themselves deeply in the mar-
              kets. In fact, Jack Schwager and I talked about it in my
              interview in *The New Market Wizards* (Harper Business,
              1992), where he said most trading systems, at least in
              terms of what they indicated, are vacuous. They are, of
              course, just different ways of describing the relationship
              of price and time. By sticking with one of those indicators
              for a while, a trader begins to get "a feel" for the markets

through that filter. Some of the more famous stories include "Trader Vic" Sperandeo spending two years in his study with stock market charts and Larry Williams studying the fine details of day trading movements.

Q: Why do you think it is so difficult for most traders to identify a true intuitive impulse and be able to trust it?

Charles: The first is emotions. Most traders, especially the young traders, are still caught up in the emotionality of trading. To pay attention to the subtleties of their feelings, or any other sense, about the markets is something that is simply not available to them. And then there's the ability, or rather inability, to act on that intuition. Remember, by its very unconscious nature, the intuition will not include all the steps and logic of how it was arrived at. Is it a real insight or just wishful thinking? Has this happened before? How much can be risked on an unplanned thought or feeling? Oops, the opportunity is gone. Now it's feel bad about missing another opportunity, thereby blocking any further intuitions until calming down, hours, days, or weeks later.

The second is that most traders have limited their intuitions to predicting market moves. Looking into the future is one kind of intuition, and there are many others. The interviews with market wizards prove this page after page. It was the intuition of Ed Seykota to write a computer program that traded and, in the process, invent program trading. It was the intuition of the CRT founders, Joe and Mark Richie, to use computers to get a little bit of everything instead of trying to get a lot of one thing. It was the intuition of Jim Rogers to not use computers and go where no one else was going, basically inventing emerging market funds in his wake. It was the intuition of Paul Tudor Jones to use analogies to previous markets to understand the current ones. It's been the intuition of other wizards to notice that assets allocation was the key to their trading success. Many famous traders talk about the importance of all aspects of money management. Young traders seldom want to hear any of this. It's not exciting. It's not sexy. It's not like catching a big move in the S&P. The point is, valuable intuitions are found far beyond the bounds of market indicators. I think these are intuitions because, in most cases, these market wizards were the first to apply their approach. How did they know to go there instead of doing what everyone else was doing? Intuition. It's available in every aspect of trading, and for many market wizards, that has made all the difference.

Q: Charles, how does this relate to the trader wishing to develop this kind of intuition from your perspective?

Charles: I'm reminded of a trader I know who was at a cocktail party a few years back and found himself arguing persuasively that the U.S. was going to win the Gulf War in a very short period of time. As he was speaking, he realized the market implications of what he was saying. He was already long in the U.S. stock market, but he went into his office the next day and put on a very large position following that intuition, which proved to be right. Intuition comes out of paying attention to those moments and acting on them.

There's a third point. So far, we've examined emotions as blocks to noticing intuitions, and the fact that an intuition may come from an area of trading that didn't seem important, but is. In both cases, we considered the intuitions to be accurate insights. What about misleading intuitions, insights that aren't? The kind that are most likely to come into the minds of young traders. That youthful feeling of certainty that you've just solved an 'impossible' puzzle, when in fact, you've slipped and missed a step.

In brain science research, these mistaken intuitions are called "cognitive illusions." How they came about is the story of our history. Not suprisingly, our brains were designed for prehistoric conditions. Our ancestors needed to decide what was food (and what wasn't), how to hunt, when to attack (and retreat), and all the rest, and to do so in a hurry. Those who survived learned to reach these conclusions with very little evidence because there often wasn't a second chance. A certain kind of intuition got very well developed. Emotionally biased, ownership oriented, based on a few representative examples, and in accordance with the status quo, this thinking is part of all of us. Now our brains are examining highly complex phenomena with these same "quick draw" prehistoric brains.

Take a regular coin. Flipping it several times, say it comes up HHTTHHTTH. What will the next flip be? What are the odds? Most of us know the odds are 50/50 that it will come up heads, but how do you feel? This is a cognitive illusion. It's also known as the fallacy of small numbers. There simply isn't enough data there to build a pattern, yet the young trader is often looking for patterns that aren't there. It's the same cognitive illusion when the market keeps going up and the public can't see that it will ever stop. After years of experience, the expert trader, who, you'll recall, has at some point radically reorganized his intuitions, will recognize the deeper patterns and plan accordingly.

Q: Are you saying, in essence, that intuition is some sort of highly refined probability thinking?

Charles: Not just probabilistic thinking, though that is certainly a part of it. More generally, it is not accepting the easy solution. There may be an easy solution, but it's being willing to look at it and consider what else might be there— and where else could this go. And paying attention to all the information that is available.

Q: So intuition is a deeper insight into what is not patently obvious. And that is why young traders can't rely on it?

Charles: Let me give you an example that is a real and prevalent characteristic of young traders. I'm going to make the analogy to something that has been well tested, and some people are going to disagree with it when they read it. It's the idea of hot hands in basketball. Well, there is no such thing!

Now, players will swear by it, and fans will swear by it, but by every statistical measure, there are no hot hands!

the "hot streaks" are well within expected probabilities. There are, of course, emotional biases, and these are real. These same biases come out when trading the markets. If you have been winning in your trades for a while, then you start to feel like you're a winner. You will take on a little bit bigger size or a little bit more risk. Whereas, if you have been losing for a while, you can start to feel like a loser. You tend to get a little hesitant and edgy: "Well, I won't take this trade." These are well-documented emotional habits, and the young trader falls into them quite easily. The more experienced expert trader begins to see that the reason the markets gyrate is precisely because so many players are falling into these and other natural human tendencies.

Charles, could you talk a little bit more about the development of intuition, about the soil that is necessary, you know, to grow intuition?

Charles: In order to develop as a trader, it's important for the novice to get beyond as many of the cognitive illusions as he can. He will need to create situations that will do that for him. The number of traders who have cut their money management teeth by gambling is as thick as a deck of cards. Young traders who have the opportunity to watch and interact with an experienced mentor may be able to avoid some bad habits and internalize some good ones.

It is important to know how much is involved in becoming an expert trader: thoroughly knowing your markets, your indicators, your money management, your approach, and yourself. I am always amazed as I study trading how much more there is to know. I was trading for two years before I realized the importance of bet size. I have a list of "must knows" I show traders. When they look at it, they typically respond with, "That's a lot of work." And I say, "Yes, you have to be passionate about this!"

If you have avoided the cognitive illusions, and really learned and applied what you need to know as a trader, then you are trading with a confidence based on competence. You are in the state of mind where you are trading your system and not your emotions. Now, you can actually pay attention to what feelings you are getting. You can try out scenarios in your mind. You can do so with a sense of detachment that allows you to test them out. Does this feel right? Does that have a good possibility of working out? What haven't I thought of? You are now capable of letting your imagination step in because you are not driven by fear or greed.

Q: According to your point of view, what is the relationship between intuition and confidence?

Charles: I think that people often mistake self-confidence for intuition, as in "I'm confident, therefore I am sure of this." Confidence is the belief in the likelihood of one's success. As a species, I think we have survived some of our darker moments because of this, but it doesn't mean that we've made good decisions. Being confident in one's likelihood of success and being confident of a particular trading position are quite different. The first will see you trade another day. The second, if insisted upon, will end your trading. The markets are always right. In terms of intuition, a person who feels confident is in a position to pay more attention to those subtle inner signals: ideas, thoughts, or feelings.

Q: Let's talk some more about these subtle inner signals: ideas, thoughts, and feelings, as you refer to them. How is a trader to know when he is having an intuition? In your way of thinking about things, are intuitions somehow different from the rest of our experiences?

Charles: I can answer this question quite specifically, though first I'll need to conduct a little NLP training. One of the first discoveries Richard Bandler and John Grinder, the co-founders of NLP, made was that people think in terms of their senses. That is, when we think about something, what we're thinking about we see, hear, feel, taste, and smell in our mind. Think of a rose, and in your mind you'll see a rose and perhaps smell it. If I ask you what color it is, you have to look. It's the same with a market. Do you see the chart or quote screen and hear yourself reading the price? While scientists don't know exactly how all our neurons do this, it's now generally agreed that we do. Every thought is "represented" mentally with our senses. NLP goes further to say that each of us has developed one of our senses more than the others. For example, someone might have a very well-developed visual sense (and therefore sees a lot of subtly different colors and details), with a much less developed kinesthetic sense (the NLP term for sensations and feelings). Another person might have a well-developed auditory (sounds and words) sense and a less developed visual sense, and so on. It might surprise you how this affects a trader's choice of system. Traders with a well-developed visual sense will be drawn to pattern recognition–based trading, that is, charts, graphs, and other ways of picturing the markets. Traders with a well-developed auditory sense will want a more rule-based system. Traders with a well-developed kinesthetic sense are often most comfortable on the exchange floors. If they move upstairs, they often have to scramble to develop new ways to continue to get the "feel" of the markets. While a trading station might have all the "bells and whistles," it's very "enlightening" to see what an individual trader pays attention to. Each trader will nonverbally show you his preference for his most developed sense.

How we come to have these sensory distributions is a matter of speculation without conclusions. As a rule of thumb, a person's most developed sense will be used in his career, while his least developed sense will be used in his hobby, avocation, or recreational activities. Now the kicker to all this, and the answer to your original question: How does a trader know when he is having an intuition? How is it different from the rest of his experience? The answer is: an individual's intuition will come from his least developed sense. That is to say, if someone's thinking is well developed in terms of pictures and words, he will typically get intuitions in the form of feelings. I should add that this is a common expression of intuition in our Western industrial culture and that other cultures have other combinations.

Q: Charles, when you talk about people's senses, could you develop that a little bit more? Are you saying that some people are more apt to image things visually rather than hear or feel their thoughts?

Charles: Yes. Say I ask you, "What's your favorite market?" If you are more developed visually, you will see your paper charts laid out with marks on them, or you will see your trading screen. Another trader might hear the sounds of the market or recite the prices for the last couple of days. Another trader might feel the energy around him as a participant on an exchange floor.

Q: And according to this view, you are saying that intuition generally comes to that trader through a sense that is not the developed one for that individual?

Charles: It's one with which he has the least facility. Consider, if it's easy for you to see pictures in your mind's eye and change them around, then if you got an insight or intuition in that sense, you would probably ignore it. It's just another picture. But if your feelings are not so easy for you to change, and you get a strong feeling about a market, it will be much more difficult for you to ignore it. As a rule of thumb, if you like charts, your intuitions will come in feelings or phrases. If you are rule based and reciting prices, you'll get an insight or a feeling about a market. If you already trade on your feelings, you'll see something in a market or get an idea (in words). Of course, there are exceptions to this, and the exceptions will be regular and patterned within a specific individual.

It's quite interesting that you can know people are talking about their intuitions in the way they describe them. Someone will get a flash. Another will hear a phrase repeated over and over again in his mind, and yet another will get a feeling he just can't ignore. Notice that in each case, the sensory message was spontaneous and amplified out of the ordinary. In the examples I just gave, the variety of amplifications included intensity, repetition, and persistence. Our unconscious minds are often trying their best to let us know if only we would look, listen, or feel.

Q: Charles, are there different kinds of intuition?

Charles: Well, there are definitely different sensory biases a person can have. As I said earlier, if someone visualizes easily and is facile with language, then that individual's intuitions are most likely to come as feelings. It is well known among the Native American cultures, which are more body- and feeling-oriented cultures, that their sources of inspiration were visions that would come to them in a flash or hearing voices that revealed truths. Now as far as trading is concerned, this "hearing voices" is not like your dog telling you to buy the Deutsche mark, but rather the idea that something is revealed to you. You hear yourself saying, "Look at that chart again." You were just flipping through your charts and an inner voice tells you to look at that chart again. This is an intuition. This is a moment to which to pay attention. You are being offered a gift. There is something there that you didn't see consciously. A part of you saw it. Give that part its due. Look at that chart. Maybe it's nothing. Maybe it's the next big thing. Give it a chance.

When I decided to get deeply involved in modeling traders, I went to see Pete Steidlmayer and used NLP to model him. To share some of that, which I haven't done before, after the course, I imagined him behind me as my advisor when I started trading. I could feel his hands on my shoulders, not that Pete ever did that with me, mind you, but in my mind, I would be trading with this mental image of him. Over the following weeks, I increasingly got a sense of him moving inside of me. It started out as voices, saying, for example, "Pay attention here." "Okay." "Watch that." I hadn't planned to say these things. They were just said to me. Eventually, I could just look at a chart using Market Profile® and get an internal image of the market movement and a feeling about that market. That was a way of developing that skill in myself.

Q: So for you, in that instance, the intuition derived from integrating the best qualities of somebody else into your own trading style.

Charles: I think that is what happens when people get a really good mentor. It is the same way we learn in other business environments. People begin to dress like their mentors, buying the same kind of suits and same kind of shoes and drinking the same drinks. So, too, the young trader will take on some of the behavioral habits of the more experienced trader. In doing that, they are really signaling to themselves, to their unconscious mind, to think and act like him. As the young trader mimics his experienced mentor, he begins to take on some of those thoughts and get similar mental containers, if you will, to store the intuitions that he is building.

Q: Sports pychologists and coaches often say that the more conscious you become of the exact things you're doing in your particular sport, the more inhibiting the effect. I'm wondering as far as intuition goes, from your point of view, does that same thing happen? As you become more conscious of your intuitive impulse, and you try to make sense of it, that is, change it from a right-brain activity into a left-brain activity, supplying categories and analyzing that experience, does it take you out of the game? Does it diminish intuition as an effective trading tool?

Charles: First of all, analyzing an intuition and utilizing it are two different things. You can have one without the other, though as you note, most people don't appreciate that, nor do they realize they are most often analyzing without utilizing.

         If a trader takes his intuition, an unconscious competence, and tries to figure it out with a conscious process, he will diminish it. So the question becomes, How do you develop intuition, that is, an unconscious competence, while leaving it unconscious? For those readers acquainted with NLP, this may seem contrary to the NLP idea of modeling. The issue here is code congruence. A model must be congruent, that is, aligned, with what is being modeled. A dissected frog may have been a frog, but it's essence is gone. NLP is interested in modeling the essence.

Q: Exactly. So what's the answer?

Charles: Remember my original definition of intuition? "You got a solution, and you don't know how you got there." The essence of intuition is that leap. To develop your intuition, the first step is to keep a dated trading journal of your thoughts, feelings, ideas, and insights, that is, your leaps. Prediction in hindsight is one of the most common cognitive illusions. You may say to yourself at a later date that you knew the dollar was going to crash. Then look in your trading journal. If it's not in there, your mind has played a trick on you. We are all rewriting history. Another thing is that your mind will be selective about the trades you remember. Your trading journal will help keep the record somewhat straighter.

Q: Charles, in your view, how does one know if an intuition is true?

Charles: Notice how, when, and where you "receive" your intuitions. Do they come as feelings, pictures, or words? Compare your intuitions with your ordinary experiences. Remember, they are often amplified in some way. How are they different? Are they bigger, stronger, louder, smaller, softer? Do they come at a certain hour or during an activity? As you build up a history of these in your journal, patterns will emerge. You'll begin to discover things you can do to deliberately encourage your intuition, such as taking a break at a certain time, playing certain music, talking out loud, or even doodling. From time to time, review your intuitions, whether you acted on them or not, to see how they have worked out and the ones that didn't. Are they in different places in your mind's eye, ear, and body? What else is different? You'll find you can continue to refine these distinctions. This activity will increase your confidence in following certain intuitions because now you have reliable cues and a trustworthy track record.

Q: Charles, can you think of a specific example of a trader who you helped to develop his intuition? Could you tell us something about the trader? What he was like before and after? What the experience was like for him? How did your work with him improve his trading?

Charles: As you know, traders very often engage me when they are in a period of transition. For example, moving from an exchange floor to upstairs, or from trading their own accounts to setting up a team, or to managing accounts. In these situations, I am called in, not to develop anyone's intuition per se, but to facilitate clear thinking and effective action that will allow the traders to get certain internal processes optimized for themselves and others.

In the case of the first trader I am thinking of, it started out as a modeling of his trading strategy. While his approach was highly mechanical, he made it a habit to have other traders around, particularly novices. After clarifying his trading strategies with me, he realized that it was important to know what a novice trader would do in particular trading situations. He literally had this as a step in his trading strategy. He felt this was a significant insight, because once he understood what a novice would do, he wouldn't do it. It might be the way a novice would get scared, or try to get some more out of the markets when it really wasn't there, or not capture enough profit. I helped him realize he could build a novice in his head. After all, he had seen enough of them. He knew how they thought, so he could avoid their mistakes without their physical presence. His intuition of having novice trading patterns around him as a safety check became an explicit step in his strategy. Now he knew exactly what not to do.

Another case was a trader who had been a very powerful presence on the Chicago Board of Trade in the bond

market. He was a real battler in the markets, a very physically aggressive trader. As he moved upstairs, he realized that he didn't have his hands on the market in the
same way that he did before. In working with me, we
discovered that he had a strong identification with some
of the great generals in history. We began to develop this
to his advantage and shifted his trading from making individual trades into military campaigns. His intuitions
began to shift from those of an individual soldier on the
battlefield to those of a general monitoring the unfolding
market movements. He discovered that he began to see
the markets in larger time frames, and how more variables affected the unfolding events.

Q: His intuition was taking him to war!

Charles: Yes, that's one of his metaphors and it works for him.

Q: Are there specific exercises that you could recommend for
            developing intuition?

Charles: Yes. Begin by acknowledging them. Intuitions are leaps.
            They are spontaneous thoughts or feelings that just come
            to us. Most of us are so busy and goal oriented these days
            that we think we don't have time for daydreams, reveries,
            or wondering; the fertile ground of intuitions. So rather
            than pushing them away and trying to stay on track,
            pause a moment and give your intuitions some room. Let
            them develop. Write them down. Encourage them by
            thanking them for showing up, no matter how bizarre or
            useless they appear to be. This is especially important for
            men in our culture, since there isn't very much encour-
            agement to trust our intuition.

            For some people, and I hate to sound like I'm recom-
            mending this, intuition comes forward when they light
            up a cigarette or sit down with a drink. It is not so much
            the nicotine or the alcohol, but rather that the person is
            inviting himself to break away from his day-to-day con-
            cerns and just wonder about things. For other people, it
            comes while jogging or working out. You can begin to
            direct this process once you notice this.

Also, you must be willing to act both with and against your intuitions and record the results. Sometimes you need to act with them, you want to go with them, but on the other hand, find out what happens when you go against your intuition. Let yourself know you are going to do this. Most people find the results more than interesting. Finally, encourage your intuitions by "wondering." Go wash your car, or mow the lawn, or do any other "mindless" chore. With your brain on break, your mind is free to wonder. Then notice what comes to mind and write it down. Be especially willing to pay attention to the oddball ideas.

Q: Charles, you refer to them as oddball ideas. Do you think this is a characteristic of intuition?

Charles: Whenever I give trading seminars, some trader will come up to me and say he was really convinced he had a good position in a market, but when he called a friend, he discovered his friend was taking the opposite position, and suddenly he wasn't so sure. Meanwhile, I'm thinking to myself, "Good, you want him to take the opposite because you need people on the other side of your trade." You see, I take that kind of thing as a good sign. Considering that 90 percent of the people in this business eventually lose money, if you go with the crowd, you are going the wrong way. So, yes, to answer your question. I think that intuition is often outside of what would normally "fit," or at least it's seeing things from a different angle. Lately, I have been conducting a study of traders who have achieved really great results, and I have found almost everyone of them were pioneers of some new method or approach. They were the ones willing to be the first out there, to test what appeared to others to be oddball ideas. These traders made a lot of money being the pioneers.

Q: From your experience, would you say that people who are in touch with their intuition are more successful in trading?

Charles: The people that I know who are most successful at trading are passionate about it. They fulfill what I think is the first requirement: developing intuitions about something they care about deeply, in this case, trading. They are the people who study years of charts, or commodity annuals, or the intricate politics of a country, or the international movement of capital. They develop a deep knowledge of whatever form of analysis they use. Out of that passion and knowledge, their trading ideas, insights, and intuitions emerge.

Q: Charles, do you think one can become a successful trader without being intuitive?

Charles: The case that I've been making here is that intuition is natural to all of us. All of our ideas start as intuitions. It's sort of like the husband who says his wife is the one who has intuition, he just has feelings. I think all of us have intuition to some extent. It's a question of how much we are willing to acknowledge it. I think denying one's intuitive sense can get one into trouble. Yet I know some very system-oriented traders who have made a good living on something that doesn't look intuitive at all. But to become great, really great in anything, I think one draws deeply on one's unconscious capacity for intuition.

There's a tradition in judo that is not practiced any more. It used to be that you made your way up through the different levels—white belt, brown belt, black belt (and other colors in the United States), and so on—and finally, when you got to the highest level, your black belt would be taken away and you'd be given your white belt again. This was the point at which your every movement through the world was expression of the art; that is, you yourself had become the art. It reminds me of what Tom Baldwin said when I asked him about his metaphors of trading. Was it a game, or a puzzle, or a person, or a war, or what? He mused about it for a moment, said he'd been through all of those, and finally he said, "Trading is life." For him, the intuitions of the market and what he's about have merged completely. They are one and the same.

This is not a mystical thing I'm talking about. It's like an experienced mechanic who loves cars. Say he's been working on high-performance automobiles for years. You bring one of those cars to him, and he can just see, hear, feel, and smell the way it runs. He gets a sense of it. He knows where to look and what he needs to do. I think the same applies to the master trader who looks at his charts and his trading system and realizes one day that it's not the same market anymore. What looks like magical insights and intuitions are born of a craft. They result from the mastery of the craft.

Q: I know there are traders who are reading this and thinking to themselves, Okay, sounds great, but what does this have to do with a channel breakout? My response always is, a channel breakout can be more or less than a channel breakout! A lot has to do with insight and intuition at that moment in time, and what is available. How much are you willing to trust yourself at the moment the market trips off your indicator? I am just wondering, Charles, in a more practical sense, how can traders utilize intuition to enhance their current trading?

Charles: I have an expression that I sometimes share with traders. "You know what you know, and you don't know what you don't know." After people get over the feeling that I am just trying to be clever, they recognize the point: until you've experienced it, you just don't know!

There's a quality that's very important in seeing a trader through this. The traders I know who are very successful share a willingness to be wrong or, to quote the old phrase, "cut their losses." The mistake that the novice or younger trader makes is wanting to cut losses to zero in order to never take a loss, thereby never trading at all or losing it all. What I find with the traders who make money is that there is always a willingness to go back and try out another idea and take a little loss to try it, knowing that the successes will pay for themselves. With that kind of a mind set, you pursue your intuitions and you develop them. It is not that intuition is a something, but rather, it's a process, a skill in us, that can be developed, like driving a car or anything else.

Q: I think Mark Douglas makes this point in a very convincing way when he asks traders to recall the first time they ever saw a price chart and to relate what they remember seeing at that moment. Most traders report just seeing random vertical lines or some such thing. However, over time most people who have been working with charts now see a completely different thing. They see specific patterns, down trends; in short, they can identify opportunities. Now what has changed? The answer isn't the price chart!

Charles: That is exactly the point I was making. Intuition is born of experience.

Q: As an example, the great traders will wait for a channel breakout, in fact expect it. Then it comes and they don't take that particular trade. When asked why they didn't take action, they will simply say something like it didn't feel right or it didn't smell right! That kind of intuition in my experience can come only from having put in the time and making the deep commitment that trading requires.

Charles: I would also describe that simply as a willingness to be wrong. I mean, how many incredible insights does one need in a lifetime? Are you making use of the ones that you're currently getting? I am reminded of an experience that Ed Seykota shared with a group. He said that when he looks at a market that everyone else thinks has exhausted its up trend, that is often when he likes to get in. When I asked him how he made this determination, he said he just put the chart on the other side of the room, and if it looked like it was going up, then he would buy it. Upon hearing this story, a number of the traders gasped out loud, but, of course, this trade was seen through the eyes of someone with deep insight into the market behavior.

Q: Some years ago I interviewed a very well-known S&P

trader who also happens to be an accomplished musician. I recall asking him how he knew when it was a good time to enter the market. His answer was that he played his S&P price chart and if it sounded right, he knew it was the right trade to be in. The interesting thing, I believe, is not whether it really works, but the fact that it really works for him!

Charles: Linda Bradford Raschke, with whom I appeared at a conference recently, also has a strong musical background, and that same kind of pattern recognition skill came through. As you point out, recognizing a pattern based on experience is where intuition comes through. This is true of every market wizard I've studied. Their trading approach developed out of a natural love of something earlier in their lives. For Linda, it is music. For Ed Seykota, it is mathematics and systems. For Jim Rogers, it is history and current events. For Richard Dennis, it is (baseball) statistics. Each has said, unequivocally, that the markets pay them to do what they love, and these are only some of the well-known examples. The point for the younger trader is clear: don't abandon your past when you go into trading, embrace it. It's where your intuition will find your pot of gold. And, remember, an intuition may be related to a pattern in a chart, or your overall trading style, or your asset allocation strategy, or something else entirely.

Q: Charles, in our last conversation we spoke in depth about the state of mind and strategy that are required for successful trading. How do state of mind and strategy, in your view, relate to intuition?

Charles: Well, to paraphrase Thomas Edison, I think that intuition is 99 percent perspiration and 1 percent inspiration. We've already covered the importance of a balanced state of mind, so let's look at strategy. First, you want your trading strategy to be smooth, streamlined, and unconscious; something that you can do easily. If it is gummed up, if you are hesitant, or frustrated, or internally divided, don't do it! You will need to do some work on your strategy first so that you do it easily. Then, I think intuition comes easily, if you let it. It is not something that you need to grunt or grovel or moan to give birth to. Rather, it is something that will just come to you out of that 99 percent effort to master your craft: trading the markets.

Q: So basically, Charles, what we are left with is a concept of intuition that is the result of a lot of enthusiasm and passion but also a lot of hard work. It is like what Woody Allen said about life: 90 percent of it is showing up. You really have to put in the work and learn the skill well, and as a result of that, you will be available to understand what your own physical and psychologic reactions are to that experience.

One of my favorite quotes is from Thomas Edison. He is reported to have said, "Recognizing opportunity is so difficult for most people because it goes around disguised in overalls, looking like hard work!" One does have to put in the time. Funny how, when you do that, opportunity reveals itself!

Charles, in your opinion what are the steps that are necessary to becoming a successful trader?

Charles: I've given whole interviews on just that question. In summary, I believe there are five areas that need to be addressed and developed in order to insure the highest likelihood of success: (1) market indicators—one's edge; (2) trading strategies, including money management; (3) emotional management; (4) beliefs that support success; and (5) a metaphoric mind-set in which you are the winner. To get started, though, there is only one requirement: to care passionately about trading! I have told several novices that the desire to become a trader is pretty much like the desire to become a Hollywood actor. There are so many people who want to do it, and the chances of success are so slim, that if you want to do anything else, go do that now! If, on the other hand, you feel you must do this, you've come to the right place.

Chapter Six

Edward Allan Toppel

Edward "Eddie" Allan Toppel is an independent trader and long-term member of the Index and Options Market (I.O.M.) of the Chicago Mercantile Exchange. He is a former stock trader with extensive experience trading futures and options. He is the author of Zen in the Markets *(Warner, 1994).*

Q: Eddie, how did you first become interested in markets?

Eddie: I was in high school and my mother worked for a brokerage firm. She would come home and talk about these exciting guys, traders. Also while I was in college, I traded some stocks, just investing and, I guess you can say, got lucky. After I was graduated, I was planning to go to law school. During the summer before I had to register I got an interview and was hired by Shearson. I went to New York for several months and, when I came back, became very interested in trading options.

We're talking now about the old days when trading options was over the counter and was a pretty tricky business. I worked for Shearson for three years and then moved to Bear Stearns and worked for them for several more years. After that I bought a seat at the CBOE, and I have been a floor trader ever since.

Q: And you always traded mostly options.

Eddie: Initially, I was a market maker in Eastman Kodak and

IBM. Since 1982 I've been trading S&P futures contracts. That's all I trade in now. S&P futures and occasionally S&P options, but nothing else.

Q: Mostly in the pit?

Eddie: Yes, mostly on the floor when I'm around the exchange.

Q: What are your current trading goals?

Eddie: My current trading goals are to stop fighting this market! To follow my own advice and just go along with it. Just to keep making money. That's about it. I don't really have any specific goals other than just to be flexible. If I had to say I have to improve one thing about my trading, it is to be more flexible.

Q: How did you develop your current trading method?

Eddie: This may sound a little funny, but a long time ago, I noticed that there wasn't really anything to figure out. All you really have to do is to be able to go with what you see. I started talking to a couple of friends of mine who had started trading the S&P successfully. They said, just buy them when they're going up, and sell them when they're going down. Don't even think about it!

Although we've all discovered it's a lot easier to talk about it than to do it, I have had an experience where I actually did just that. I was able to let go and just do what had to be done. If the market was going up, I was buying, if it was going down, I was selling. I was just in rhythm. It is, as you know, an incredible feeling, to be able to let go and succeed by not having your ego interfere with your trading. To just go with the market, to go with the information exactly as you see it! The opposite experience, of course, is to hope that the market would see what I saw. In other words, let my ego dominate my trading.

Q: So would you say the basis of your buying and selling decisions is primarily catching the wave of the market?

Eddie: Right. I try never to think about the market. I don't focus on technical analysis, no fundamental analysis or anything like that. As a trader, I just go with the waves and know I can switch fast enough, when the waves break the other way!

Q: Eddie, I would like to mention here that I think your book, *Zen and the Markets*, is fascinating—obviously the result of a lot of thought and consideration about the whole enterprise of trading. Could you describe some of the mistakes that you made in trading in the past that have served as a learning experience and were a source of material for your book?

Eddie: The old idea of nonattachment! Once you're in a position and it's not working out, kick out as fast as possible without holding on to it. Detach from it. Just let go. Go the other way if you can. But at the very least, get out of the position quickly!

When my trade is in sync, I have no problems doing that. But then like most traders, I get stubborn and I just let it go too far and it gets very expensive.

Q: Well, I liked that little exercise you did in your book asking the reader to determine which of the three numbers of this series 27, 28, 29 was the largest and so on. You pretty much establish for the reader all you really have to know is which is the lowest and which is the highest, and when you can make that determination with little or no hesitation, then you are pretty much ready to trade.

Eddie: It's easy to read those numbers. It's hard to act on them because of fear and other emotions. But it's true, numbers don't lie!

Q: Does it bother you personally when you lose?

Eddie: No, it doesn't bother me at all. I can go home after the market closes and I don't take it personally.

Q: What percentage of your trades would you say are profitable?

Eddie: I would say 30 percent. That's a guess. I never really analyzed it in a very serious way. I really just try to get on the wave, so a lot of times there's a lot of chopping around before I get on and catch a wave. I will take a lot of quick losses. But hopefully I'll catch the big one.

Q: That's really the hardest for most novices to learn. Most beginners don't believe the idea that a professional trader will take that many losses in order to get on the right side of the market.

Eddie: It is very hard for people to understand that psychology.

Q: Why do you believe that you've done well as a trader?

Eddie: The one major quality that I have when I am trading well is that I can hold onto winners for a long time. I have the ability to ride them for almost the entire move. I don't take small profits because I have to make up for all those little losers that I've had. I try to hold on and ride my winners. This has been my major strength: holding onto winners when I am right and not just taking a small profit. I have some monster days when I'm right. I just ride it. The wave is long and I'm on the wave. I have the ability to hold it as long as possible.

Q: What do you believe are the characteristics of successful traders?

Eddie: Having no opinions at all. Willingness to obey the market, not to figure out what it's going to do ahead of time. Just get in there, hear the music, and start dancing to the tune and not have a preconceived idea of the tune. You know, just going with the flow of it. I have noticed one quality from trading the S&Ps because the swings are big. You must have the ability to switch when you're wrong. If you're short and the markets are going against you, turn around and go long. Even though sometimes you get whipsawed, eventually you're gonna catch the big wave.

Q: That takes a lot of confidence though, doesn't it?

Eddie: Yes, it does. You have to believe. You have to believe it's going to work. Sometimes, of course, it doesn't; but in these volatile markets it does, because it could go one way and all of a sudden it will turn the other way and go a long distance. Belief and persistence will allow you to carry the day.

Q: Could you talk a little bit about the power of belief and how that relates to trading?

Eddie: It's interesting to watch the NBA finals. Each of the coaches uses the words, "I believe we are going to win." They believe, and even the players use the word "believing." I have thought about this quite a bit and have come up with this idea. If you don't believe you can win, you probably won't win, and when you do believe you can win, you obviously stand a lot better chance. You may not win believing you can win, but I'm willing to bet you won't win if you don't believe you can win!

Q: It's very interesting. I believe there is a real power in adopting an attitude of optimism. It refers to trading and everything else. Is this consistent, Eddie, with your experience?

Eddie: You have to hope. Actually, I don't like to use the word "hope." It's a dangerous word. Very dangerous. Because you're not following your intuition. You're hoping now. I think you have to believe in yourself. That you've arrived at the right approach. That you've got control. That you're going to do the right thing when it's called for. That essentially is the difference between the traders who do well and those who don't.

Q: Let's focus on the issue of consistency. Traders talk about it all the time. How do you understand consistency as it relates to trading?

Eddie: I think the only way you can be consistent is to just be totally flexible in the market! A lot of guys are either bearish or bullish, and when the market is going their way, they're going to make money. When it's not, they're going to lose money.

    If you're totally looking for one move all the time, you're not going to be consistent. Your performance is going to be determined by the direction of the market as it relates to your opinion. I believe if you have no opinion, you will be able to be consistent because you will be able to do whatever the market shows you is the right thing to do.

Q: So if I could summarize that from your perspective, consistency is to be consistently flexible.

Eddie: Absolutely. That's the secret. You have to be flexible. If you're rigid you're not going to be consistent. Over time, you're going to get caught!

Q: Where does discipline come into this?

Eddie: Discipline. Another good word. Every trader wants to know what discipline means? It means being able to take your losses, stick to your rules, without exception, and just know that when you're going to go over a certain point, you're going to kick out when you're wrong.

If you're not disciplined, you're not going to do it. The trade will get away from you and then you're going to be stuck. You're going to be frozen.

If you're consistent and you're following your rules, you're going to be disciplined and successful. One thing is for sure: If you are not disciplined, you're going to get nailed!

Q: I would like to focus on your book for a moment. As I said earlier, I thought it was fascinating. You write, "Just remember that you are in a contest with yourself and not the market. This lack of sense of self made the Samurai warrior a powerful and formidable opponent. It takes time, understanding, and hard work to get to this point in any endeavor, especially in trading." Could you elaborate on that?

Eddie: The selfless self. It's kind of a contradiction, isn't it? In order to be able to act with consistency and discipline, you have to submerge your ego, your sense of self. You can't allow your ego to get in the way of your trading. You have to go with the market.

Q: Is that what you mean when you write, "We may win once in a while and that is bad because it bloats our ego and gives us a false sense of our missions. The river always wins, paddle with the stream."

Eddie: Basically what I meant there is that if you have an opinion and somehow the market confirms your opinion and you think you've figured it out ahead of time, that is, you knew what the market was doing, that only bloats your ego. You just got lucky and the market did what you were hoping. It was going to do whatever it was going to do no matter what you thought. If you look at how many times it doesn't do what you think it will, it should become obvious how our egos get in the way. You just have to learn to let go and follow the stream.

Q: So the goal is just to get rid of your ego and to let go.

Eddie: Right, no thoughts at all. You just don't have an opinion. An empty cup if you wish. If you're totally without an opinion, you're just there to see which way and respond to the direction of the wind. You are a selfless person, an objective participant in the market.

Q: As I'm looking at you, you're wearing your trading jacket and your acronym is EGO and I'm wondering why you chose that symbol. Why not NO EGO or something like that?

Eddie: Just to remind myself of its power over me. I chose EGO as an acronym just to remind myself that EGO is the enemy. In every endeavor, if you let your ego get involved, you're not going to see things as they are. You're just protecting yourself too much. So that's why I chose the word "ego." Just a humorous way of reminding myself. It's humorous, but really it's not humorous.

Q: Do you get any comments in the pit?

Eddie: Not anymore.

Q: Did you . . .

Eddie: Yeah, they used to call me an egomaniac.

Q: Have you gotten any other comments from traders in the pit whom you compete with on a day-to-day basis who have read your book?

Do they haze you when they see you get upset or are not following your trading prescription?

Eddie: Oh, I always hear both sides of that. I hear guys say I have to read your book again. I know one trader always tells me that some guy was trading with my book in his pocket all the time. But you hear all kinds of remarks. If you're so smart, then why are you still here? I don't make any bold personal claims in that book. I think I've attempted to tell people the way successful trading is done!

Q: Actually, the reason I ask is kind of personal. There've been a couple of times when I have been in front of the screen and I've made an obviously bad trade or what was perceived to be a bad trade by some of my colleagues, and on a number of occasions, they've turned to me and said, I know a book you can read!

Eddie: Right, I know. I'm used to that by now. The danger of writing a book like this is that people expect you to be perfect . . . to unflinchingly exemplify what you say. I made it very clear in my book that occasionally I do not do what I write about in my book. It is the ideal.

Q: You know, Eddie, one of the aspects of your book that really appealed to me was its blatant honesty. I believe you wrote that your trading career had been a wild roller-coaster ride. Could you elaborate on that?

Eddie: That's true. I had a period for a long time when I was doing exactly what I talked about in my book. This is interesting because I've talked to some professional therapists about this and how I was doing what I was telling you about. I was in an automatic zone where I was just in the stream, just doing it without thinking about it. I made a lot of money, and it was scary for a while because I couldn't do anything wrong.

Q: You were unconscious of what you were doing.

Eddie: Exactly. Whatever went on, I think can be expressed in many ways, zone, flow, but I think we all understand what we're talking about. Except I became afraid after a while. My ego jumped in and said, "Oh my God. This thing is displacing me and you're doing well." I actually thought I was becoming psychotic. I just couldn't do any wrong. And I thought something's wrong. I must have gone into . . .

Q: It's almost like your trading became purely intuitive.

Eddie: Right. I couldn't explain why I was getting in and out at these points, but it was working, and I was totally automatic and not conscious of myself, and then I got to a point where I just said, whew, this is just too scary. I shouldn't be getting this reward!

I don't know what interfered with my style, but I stopped trading like that for quite a while. In fact, I just sort of got dominated by my ego. It wanted to come back into me, and I let it do that.

Q: What did you do?

Eddie: It's a constant battle for me. I think it'll never go away. I don't think you ever get rid of your ego. You have to be aware that somewhere in the dark, in the shadows, it is lurking, waiting for an opening. And if you give it that opening, it'll seize it.

Q: As you know, the focus of this book is intuition. It sounds like this successful trading experience that you were describing was one where your trading was highly intuitive, and I can see you're nodding approvingly as I ask the question. How do you understand intuition and how do you feel intuition positively enhances the trader's performance?

Eddie: Well, that's the interesting thing about intuition. I've thought about it for a long time from various perspectives. It's the ability to act, feel good about it, and not even think about it, as we were talking about consistency and discipline before.

Q: Do you think there is such a thing as a true intuitive impulse in trading?

Eddie: I can't explain intuition, but I can give you my own understanding of what it is.

Q: What is it?

Eddie: You have a right hemisphere in your brain, and it does not talk to you in words. It talks in feelings and images and symbols. You have a left hemisphere and it talks to you in words, and it tells you what to do. It's intellectual. The right hemisphere talks in another language and that language is feelings and intuition. So when you feel something, it doesn't come to you logically.

That is how I personally understand intuition. It's the right hemisphere cooking up all this data or whatever it is and then giving you the answer, but not in a verbal message.

Q: In your opinion, Eddie, how can a trader develop his intuition?

Eddie: There are many ways. One is meditation, which I think of as a way of sanding or filing down your ego. You're never going to get rid of it, but you can reduce its size, hopefully. You're trying to reduce its existence and have the other part of your right hemisphere express itself. There is also visualization and affirmation and things like that.

Q: Are you always as serene as you have been during this interview?

Eddie: Truthfully, it's my personality, genetics, whatever. I don't know. I've always been like this.

Q: As one looks at you, you don't appear to be the stereotypical image of a trader. You know, frantic operating at a fever pitch.

Eddie: No, that's my personality. I mean I'm just very laid back. I mean I can move when I have to, but I've never been overly animated; I'm not at all manic. For the most part, I'm calm. Easy Ed, you know.

Q: Do you believe intuition is the result of commitment and hard work?

Eddie: Definitely. I mean that's the result of all the effort. What works? Hard work works! That's it! Work. Work. Work. You know, in anything, to get it without working is not satisfying for the most part, and if you don't work hard, more than likely it won't work.

I'm trying to remember what the definition of success is ... when luck meets opportunity! You know, all the preparation turns into opportunity. Intuition allows you to take advantage of all that hard work you've done. So if you let the opportunity work, you can put all the preparation to good use.

Q: What would be your words of advice to somebody who might now be going through a period of difficulty in his trading? What would you recommend?

Eddie: Get a good handle on what you're doing wrong. More than likely, you are getting locked into a belief about the market or your system. You are caught in an opinion, and you are not flowing with the market.

In reality, we all know what to do. It's just the willingness to do it that makes the difference. And for some reason or another you're not willing to make that commitment, to have the determination or persistence to follow what you know is right. For lack of a better word, my understanding is: it's your ego. It doesn't want to give up its relevance. So it interferes and then it screws you up. Your ego would rather take you down than admit it's wrong. It would rather kill you than admit it's wrong. And I mean trading, you know, people ... I mean, you've seen it. They just hold on rather than admit they're wrong, so they're being buried and their ego is what kept them from getting out or correcting their problem.

Q: In your book, you say there are basically only seven rules
            that one needs to know to be successful at trading: Never
            add to a loser; add to a winner only; let profits run; cut
            losses fast; don't pick tops; don't pick bottoms; and let
            the market make the decision, not your ego.

Eddie: Right, absolutely. Those are everybody's rules! Every-
            body knows those rules from kindergarten up. They are
            easily understood. It's just the execution of those rules
            that keeps you from doing those things.

            It's your ego at work. It's easy to add to a loser because
            you're compounding your misery. You're not admitting
            you're wrong. Your ego is saying, I'm not wrong, double
            up or triple up. You know, pretty soon, you're out of busi-
            ness if you're doing that. So we all know the rules. What
            keeps us from following the rules is really the essential
            question.

Q: Do you still enjoy trading?

Eddie: Oh, I like trading. It's a lot of fun. It's not only fun, it's
            . . . when you're doing well, it's like being in the zone.
            What a feeling that is! When you're doing everything
            right, you just let go and it's like Nirvana! When you're
            there, that's just what it's like. It's a huge feeling. For me
            that feeling is like some foods that are too rich. They're
            good, but they're rich, and you start choking on it. It's
            just too much. You start gagging! And that's really
            what happened to me. I got to a point where I started
            gagging. I got too much of it, too soon, and wasn't ready
            to handle it.

Q: Are you ready for the next wave?

Eddie: Oh, definitely. Definitely. I'll be there when it happens
            and be able to do well!

Chapter Seven

Ellen Williams, Ph.D.

Ellen Williams is a cofounder of the Soma Institute, a school developed to train health professionals in the mind-body connection. Educated in the United States and Great Britain, she has worked extensively with crisis hotlines, substance abuse therapy, and suicide counseling and for many years has specialized in working with terminally ill patients and their families.

Working with traders has been her primary interest since 1984. Dr. Williams has designed a special stress reduction program for traders, using autogenic training, a system that has been in wide use since the 1920s. These relaxation tapes provide a shortcut to a deep meditative state, leading to greater productivity and right-brain access.

Q: Ellen, could you please tell me something about your background and how you became interested in working with traders?

Ellen: Well, I was educated in England. When I returned to the States I moved to Florida and became very interested in the humanistic psychology movement. I met my husband, Bill, who was a leader in that movement and one of the first Rolfers in the United States. At this time I was studying with Ida Rolf, and Bill was trading. We were always more or less involved with very high-performance people who were, like us, interested in and involved with the body-mind connection. We were routinely working with people who were in the avant-garde of music, art, dancing, and athletics and lots of business-people, of course. We also became increasingly more interested in traders and trading.

Q: When did you come to the realization that your work in psychology could optimize trading performance?

Ellen: You know when you really tune in and listen to people, the clues that they give you and the things that they say about their trading just jump out at you. You can't miss the link.

         You'll hear them say things like "the market took my profits from me," and then you can really see that in some people there's a very primitive kind of thinking going on.

Q: They're reporting that they're not responsible. The market did it.

Ellen: I think if that's your life's view, that'll be your view in the market.

Q: When did you start working exclusively with traders?

Ellen: I want to say that at this time my work was primarily concentrated on suicidal patients, death and dying and crisis lines.

Q: You were working with clients on a psychoanalytical level, is that right?

Ellen: I was at Jackson Memorial Hospital in Miami as their thanatology person. I was training residents and interns, and I did a lot of in-service training for RNs and the whole staff, really.

         I did so much work with dying patients and with people who were at a certain point in crises, I felt I personally needed a change. I think discovering the market and working with traders was really good for me.

Q: Well, as you know, most traders consider themselves as always being in a crisis.

Ellen: Yes, but it's losing only your money, it's not like losing your life.

Q: Of course. And I'm sure it is quite difficult in a psychological sense to work in thanatology over an extended period of time.

Ellen: I think I felt after a while that I had to have a different look at things. For me it became too depressing to work exclusively with people who were in a constant morbid state.

Q: Was it a difficult transition from thanatology to working with traders?

Ellen: Well, it was not a hard transition, because I do have a pretty unorthodox view of medicine. It was difficult for me to work with physicians who were administering chemotherapy and radiation. I just don't believe that's the answer, and I had to get away from it.

Bill and I opened a school and began teaching. It was a totally different life. I still saw a few private patients who were using alternative methods. I was teaching autogenic training, my stress reduction program. You bring something from whatever you've done in the past to what it is you're doing now. Hopefully, I brought the best parts of my background and training to my current work.

Q: Ellen, as you work with traders, and I know you've worked with many over the years, is there a particular profile of the successful trader? Can you identify certain specific characteristics of the high performers?

Ellen: Yes. They're independent thinkers, and they are people who know to manage their time and structure their lives. They don't require a lot of rules. They are comfortable in their own skin. People who have had a highly regimented existence have difficulty adjusting to the trading environment. For instance, the traders who seem to have the toughest time are doctors. They feel since they went to medical school and they succeeded in their chosen profession they ought to be able to do anything. But trading is quite different.

Q: Do you believe that is because doctors are not used to the ambiguity and psychological paradoxes of trading?

Ellen: Well, traders can buy every book there is on trading and realize that they have to keep adjusting and in fact reject most of what they've learned in order to find a methodology or system that will work. Doctors are survivalists. They got through medical school. They got through training. Surely they can do anything if they just get enough knowledge and facts. They have a hard time because they always want facts, facts, facts. They typically don't approach trading from the perspective that you have to learn more about yourself. You have to learn how to develop your own intuition.

Q: And that works against their ability to become focused on themselves rather than facts.

Ellen: Your old doctor who diagnoses by intuition would be a much better trader than the physician who relies on every test in the world.

Q: What do you think inhibits most traders from getting the results they want from the markets, from securing the success that is within their ability to achieve?

Ellen: Let's assume that they have a great plan. Let's not go into what plan or how they developed it. Let's just look at the ability to place a trade. I mean, many traders just can't even place the trade! All they talk about all day is the fact that they missed the trade . . . "the trade," a trade that would have been the trade of . . .

Q: Yes.

Ellen: Just think about what happens to people who begin tinkering with stocks. We all know all the little things you can do to mess yourself up.

Q: I guess what you're suggesting also is that some people just do it, in the Nike sense, while others tinker. They talk about it and play with it, but all their activity and energy sort of become an excuse for not trading at all.

Ellen: Now there are gamblers who shouldn't trade at all. And I have seen a few of those people, and I've said to them, "Frankly, you know you're using this to gamble. You might as well go to the casino." The thing that is interesting about these traders is that, like most gamblers, anybody addicted to trading for this reason really trades to lose.

Q: Can you think of an example of somebody you worked with who fit that profile?

Ellen: Oh, yeah.

Q: Could you talk about him a little bit? You know, what was he like and, when you worked with him, what were some of the issues that you had to deal with, and what did you have to do with him?

Ellen: Well, the most extreme case I can think of was with a trader to whom I suggested that he not trade. That he really look into Gamblers Anonymous. He was a trader who gambled on everything, I mean everything! He was somebody who had been into horses, who lived in Vegas, and who was simply a straight-out gambler. Of course, he traded the S&P 500 and would pile on trades. He would double up and figure out new and inventive ways to keep the action going. He was an extreme case. I've really only seen one person like him.

Q: I don't know if you knew this, but on the floor of the exchange, the locals refer to the S&P 500 as the S&M. So, you know it will punish you quickly and harshly if you are of a mind to make a contribution. As you know, Ellen, there are so many people who hear about the market and they think it sounds so easy. These are the people who I think really get hurt. Maybe they know someone who has done well, but usually the market is just seen as the latest get-rich-quick scheme.

Ellen, you have made a life study of the mind-body connection. However, as you know, when most traders think of trading they don't really relate physiology to optimum performance. Could you comment about the role of physiology to optimum performance for traders?

Ellen: Of course, this is really a very lengthy thing. Physiology is a prime determining factor in everything we do in life. Why would trading be an exception? You know a lot of floor traders have demonstrated success in hockey or football. They have that particular body type. You also get people who are more lean, thin, and tall. They may tend to be more nervous in trades.

Q: I was thinking more in terms of the role of physiology in particular states of mind. To maintain and condition one's ability to stay focused, to stay disciplined.

Ellen: Well, I think before, when you asked me what is the profile of a successful trader, I would add to what I said that it would be the person who is definitely in touch with his body. The trader who is aware of his pulse rate and his body, who's conscious of what he eats and its effects. The more you are aware of everything you do, the more able you will become to create states of mind that will produce optimum trading performance.

Q: I know one of the concepts that underlies your stress reduction series is that a clear mind and reduced anxiety while trading produces better concentration and consequently better results. Isn't it interesting that for most traders this is not a key component of their own trading. Yet when you speak to the very best traders, they acknowledge this is the essence of their trading!

Ellen: Absolutely! The best traders condition themselves psychologically and physically for success. They have running programs. They go to the gyms. They meditate. They are careful about what they eat. In short, they take excellent care of themselves.

What the autogenic training tapes do is they first deal

with things like your pulse and then show you how to achieve states of deep relaxation.

Q: Ellen, could you say something about how you first began to use the autogenic tapes with traders, and then give a little background of their development for people who are unfamiliar with autogenic training.

Ellen: Autogenic training was developed on the continent in the 1920s. It's still in use throughout Europe. Various methods have been used in this country, but I've tried to keep my tapes as pure as possible. The tapes are designed for people to achieve a form of self-hypnosis so that they are not dependent on anyone. Within ten to twenty seconds you can put yourself into a state of deep relaxation. It takes six weeks to complete the entire program.

I've taught this training since the 1960s, and I've been using the tapes now for quite a few years. I used them first with athletes and then went on to work with them for traders.

Q: When did you first start using them with traders?

Ellen: I think it was probably in '84 or '85.

Q: Can you think of a trader who used your training system and how it improved his trading?

Ellen: I'm thinking of one trader who really needed them because he was much too intense about his trading. He was a competitive tennis player and ended up winning a tournament after the first two weeks of using the tapes. I think this experience convinced him that the tapes could positively benefit his trading. He learned how to monitor his pulse and breathing to create a feeling of deep calm and freedom from anxiety.

It's important that traders realize how their anxieties control all their behaviors, everything from eating to trading.

Q: Just worrying about their trading, the anxiety takes over.

Ellen: That's why they eat, as a way to tap down that worry.

That hole needs to be filled, and people use food, drugs, or alcohol. All kinds of things.

Q: Ellen, do you think trading at the highest level is a mechanical skill or more of a right-brain activity, more of an aesthetic activity?

Ellen: I think you can look at trading as an art form. Let's face it, you're really going to the source of things when you trade, aren't you?

I think that when you look at things at that level, it's much more than mechanical competence. If you look at a great painter or at a great musician, they've had to learn technique; but once it is learned, they never think about the techniques. In fact, if they do, it gets in the way. Accordingly, trading is a right-brain function. Anything you do at the highest level is: swimming, running, all kinds of things.

Q: It's very interesting that you mention that because I was speaking with Richard McCall the other day. He is a martial arts expert and a psychologist specializing in optimum performance. He too mentioned the idea of trading as an art form, very much like the martial arts. I think there's a lot of similarity to your point of view.

Ellen: I think it has to be considered from that perspective, but you also must remember that you can't get to that art form without learning the basics. You're going to have to know how to draw before you can produce a masterpiece.

Q: I think in trading this is an issue that really doesn't get enough recognition. So much emphasis is placed on the mechanical side alone. The fact is that becoming an intuitive trader requires unbelievable commitment, dedication, and discipline.

Ellen: I don't think anything else works. You have to have that tenacity and one other important thing, natural inclination. I think you have to have an affinity for trading to be successful. I don't think anybody can do anything well just because they decide to do it. I think you need to find what fits you. I go back to the training of doctors. You'll meet young men in medicine, and they'll say I'm going to do this and I'm not going to do that. When you do your clinical work, you'll find soon enough where you sit. You can't make an emergency room doctor. I mean you really have to crave it. I think that's true in trading too. You really have to crave it.

Q: Ellen, in your view, then, intuition is a way of getting in touch with one's natural affinity? Is that a correct way of saying it?

Ellen: Yes, I think that your intuition probably comes into play much faster when you are at the place you need to be and doing what you need to do.

Q: From your viewpoint, Ellen, are there different kinds of intuition?

Ellen: I don't know how you mean "kinds."

Q: Richard McCall referred to two kinds of intuition, sensory and extrasensory. But I think that was just his own personal take on it. I'm wondering if you could elaborate on your personal understanding of intuition and how you think successful traders are tapping into their intuition in ways that other traders can't, or don't?

Ellen: Well, personally, I think when I don't pay attention to my intuition, I usually regret it. I think we live in a funny world where feelings are not valued as much as facts. I think that's a shame because you can know a lot of facts, but if you can't apply your feelings to them, the facts aren't going to work for you as well as for someone who does have great intuition.

I just think it has to do with the whole educational system that we've grown up with. Truth always has to be articulated. We grow up being taught that there's more truth to a category or a paradigm than there is to a poem.

I think you'll frequently hear the traders say, "I knew" that trade. I knew it when I got in that it would make money. Or I knew that it was going to work out well.

Conversely, you will hear them say, "I knew I shouldn't have taken that trade." And that's what you must work with. Why do traders ignore those warnings? The purpose of my tapes is to get traders in touch with their feelings.

Q: I loved what you said in the beginning of your stress reduction tape. It really struck a cord with me, and it's something that I felt in the past when I have tried to meditate. You begin your tape series by saying that for many Westerners the idea of relaxing through meditation is in itself a source of anxiety. I said to myself, "How true that is." You really put your finger on why it is so difficult for many traders to use this technique.

Ellen: Well, that's why I begin with a very simple goal: my right arm is heavy . . . you have no other goal. Thoughts go racing through our minds. You just come back to my right arm is heavy and eventually everybody will get heavy. For some people it takes a couple of weeks. Other people can do it in a day.

Q: I found its benefit almost immediate. I mean I just got such a strong feeling when I did it. The sense of deep relaxation was very strong and soothing. I thought it was just a terrific exercise.

Ellen: I think it works because it's simple. I also find that with a lot of traders I like to work with dreams. I like to get them to record their dreams and talk to me about them. Your dreams will tell what you need to know.

Q: Ellen, are you saying as a trader becomes more aware of his dream life or what his dreams reveal about his intuitive side he will begin to see improvements in his actual trading?

Ellen: The dreams generally illustrate where a person is or where they want to be.

        I'm thinking of one person whose dreams revealed that he was always on a trip. He was always going off somewhere or on a train. He was on a plane having trouble getting somewhere, which is, of course, not an uncommon dream. The idea of being unable to reach a particular goal. In the case of the one person I'm thinking of, the dream resolved the conflict in a very strange way. The person stated his usual dream of going to get on a train, being late, and encountering problems. But what distinguished this dream was he just turned around, left the train station, got into his own car, and went home. And it was a very significant dream. That for him was the realization that he was in the driver's seat. He was able to control this seemingly endless stream of losses (endless problematic travel without a successful destination). I think that was one example of how understanding your dream and then using this information could make a tremendous difference.

Q: So once you brought this to his awareness, he was able to take steps to improve his performance.

Ellen: Yes, he gained more control over his trading and the kind of trades he would be involved in.

Q: From your experience, does the awareness alone usually change behavior?

Ellen: I think the awareness leads to changes. I think the awareness leads to the courage to make decisions to change.

I would like to make another point. A lot of traders are very unhappy in their relationships because they have significant others who don't approve of, or understand, trading. They think trading is nothing more than gambling. They say things like "Trading is too risky." "Why are you sitting at home all day throwing away your money?" I see and hear a lot of that!

Q: What do you think about this notion that we hear quite often at conferences that to be a successful trader one has to lead a totally balanced life?

Ellen: I think that many people think that if their life were totally balanced, they would just do great. You know, as if I just had a clean desk that would make all the difference!

I don't think that has anything to do with it. I mean, I think if you don't keep records and you don't know what you did yesterday and you don't update your charts, that's just a pretty poor way to run a business.

There are lots of people who trade very successfully that lead pretty wild lives.

Q: Exactly.

Ellen: But, let's be clear on one thing. In order to trade successfully, you've got to have discipline. You've got to update and review charts and look back at how things have been going. But you don't have to lead some monastic existence of eating brown rice.

Q: Ellen, in your opinion, how do the top traders tap into their intuition?

Ellen: I think that intuition may come from paying attention. They've been attending to the market. They see what's going on. They are in tune with their own reaction, and, most important, they are operating in the moment.

The question is: Where do you go to learn this? You learn this by trial and error, don't you? And if you are a smart person, you learn by mistakes. I don't know many people who have learned a lot except by making mistakes and seeing how to avoid a particular mistake or how to change that situation enough to make it work. They watch the market, they see how markets change over time. They've absorbed that knowledge. It's like making a great sauce. You have to do it a lot. At some point you can consult with a chef, but you pretty much have to do all the work.

Q: Ellen, in your opinion, what are the steps that are necessary in becoming a successful trader?

Ellen: I think the absolutely critical factor and the least talked about is your desire to do it. That you are going to do it no matter what. I think that is your first thing and the second thing is just to learn how it works as a business.

Of course, once you have number 1, number 2 is pretty easy.

I mean a lot of this is pretty basic. Desire will make you want to accumulate knowledge. You've got to understand how this whole thing works. You talk to people. Some people are still paying a $100 commission. Sometimes I just start by asking traders where do you trade, who do you clear through, what do you pay? And it's amazing the little things you learn that they haven't really researched. Everyone wants to be a trader. How many people are willing to commit?

Q: Several years ago, Ellen, I saw a person who was so enamored with the idea of trading that I recognized it by the way he walked into my office. The first thing he did was hand me these cards that looked like they were produced by Tiffany's: under his name in bold red and gold letters were two words, futures trader. He was just in it for the sizzle. The trading played a very small part in it for him. It was just the idea that he would be identified as someone who was engaged in this industry. A trader!

Ellen: A very glamorous thing. It evokes big-money images and a very elaborate lifestyle to a lot of people, doesn't it?

I think to really be successful at trading it must be a consuming thought. If you're a writer, you've got to write even if the stores are running out of paper! You'll do it and you'll do whatever it takes. But a lot of people in life won't do what it takes. They want things, but they do not want to pay the dues. You must pay your dues, and hopefully you'll pay them joyfully. 'Cause, if it's drudgery, you won't make it either.

Q: It's hard to get people to realize that trading can be something that's almost totally effortless.

Ellen: Yes, once you've put forth the necessary effort, you do reach that point. I think the effortlessness comes because . . . it's the thing, the right thought, the right action. I think they've found their spot, and they have seen how much their intuition has played in whatever point they've reached. They've learned to trust themselves!

Q: Why is it so hard for most traders to be able to trust themselves?

Ellen: I think it's cultural. We're told that we ought to trust religion. We're told we ought to trust the government. We look at ourselves and ask, We ought to trust what? I mean, you know, these aren't things you can really trust. I think we're just told to trust outside of ourselves all the time.

Q: And, of course, the only thing you can really trust is yourself. Your feelings, your images, your dreams, your REALITY!

Ellen: And if you don't know yourself, you're adrift in trading and everything else. So it's a complicated process that once you've reached it, it looks simple. I mean once you're there, you look back and think why did this take so long? Why didn't I see this before? It was always there, right in front of me. But in trading and life you have to dig through all these layers to get to that point.

Q: Ellen, what words of advice or encouragement would you have for an aspiring trader who is really committed to becoming successful?

Ellen: First of all, truly learn everything he can about the business as a business, learn his strong points and his weak points, and most of all get in tune with who he is. Meditate every day. Keep on track. Pay attention to his dreams, his sleeping dreams, and the dreams of what he wants to achieve.

Q: Their goals and aspirations?

Ellen: Their goals and aspirations, to be very, very clear about them and also enjoy life. It is important to enjoy life because it is not meant to be a burden. It is not meant to be something to worry over. So that if you do the groundwork and then you nurture yourself, the intuition will come.

Q: I imagine a lot of people are reading this and responding to your last statement in the same way Ghandi responded to Churchill when he was visiting London and Churchill asked Ghandi, "What do you think of Western civilization?" And Ghandi's response was, "That really would be nice."

Ellen: That's true. The important point to get across to traders is that it's possible!

PART III
THE TOP TRADERS

Chapter Eight

Linda Leventhal

Linda Leventhal is a long-term independent trader and is currently a member of the International Monetary Market division of the Chicago Mercantile Exchange. She is a former member of the Mid-America Exchange and is one of the original traders in the Eurodollar market.

Q: Linda, how did you first become involved in trading?

Linda: Mostly through a suggestion by my ex-husband who was in the business. I was trained to be a teacher, and I taught first grade for six years. I received my Masters from Northwestern in reading and learning disabilities. It was a time when I was home with the kids and wasn't working for a while . . . basically, we were broke.

Q: What year was this?

Linda: 1977. I was pregnant again and we ran out of money. I decided that I just had to go back to work.

Q: Teaching?

Linda: I loved teaching, but the idea of going back wasn't something that felt good to me. You have to have a contract, and you are expected to be there every day. Trading offered the flexibility of not having to work for someone, being able to go and trade and leave whenever you wanted.

Q: So how did you get started?

Linda: I borrowed money from my mother.

Q: How much did you borrow?

Linda: I bought a seat on the Mid-America. It was ten thousand five hundred dollars. I borrowed every single penny! But the hard part was putting my kids in someone else's home.

Q: Day care?

Linda: Yes. In 1977 there really weren't any day care centers.

Q: Right.

Linda: Way back in the Middle Ages! So I took my kids to a woman who kept her kids at home. At that time I figured I had to make about fifty dollars a week to break even. It sounds funny now, doesn't it? Just fifty bucks! But that was where I was at.

    So I bought the seat on the Mid-America Exchange, and I began to trade. At that time, you really needed a tiny bit of capital to start. I started with almost nothing. I think you needed something like a thousand or fifteen hundred dollars in your account.

Q: There were no other capital requirements?

Linda: No other capital requirements, and there were no testing requirements. You didn't have to pass any kind of competency or regulatory exam. You didn't have to pass a test about trading procedures. I never clerked. I never did anything. I literally knew zero about trading. I knew nothing about economics. I never even took an economics class. I come from a family where no one had even bought stock. They put their money in the bank and that was it.

Q: Were you excited about the idea of trading?

Linda: You have to understand that I just needed to make money.

Q: Right.

Linda: At that time trading looked like a good option for me.

People told me that I had the right kind of personality to be a trader.

Q: Meaning that you were aggressive?

Linda: Yeah. I was always pretty aggressive. I have always been the kind of person that if I put my mind to something I take charge. I will accomplish it.

Q: What would be an example of that?

Linda: I don't know. Maybe grades in college. It was not hard for me to figure out what I needed to do to get an A in class. And I did it. I would just keep getting A's.

Q: Right. So you pretty much thought with trading that you would just identify what you needed to do and then go out and rack up a lot of trading A's.

Linda: Well, that's what I had done in the past.

Q: But trading . . .

Linda: Trading was very different from anything I had ever done in the past. I learned it was not as easy as it looked, by a long shot.

Q: What was your initial experience like?

Linda: It was awful. Just awful! I had eight months of diarrhea. I lost weight. It's true. I was sick to my stomach, but I loved it, and I knew I could be successful. Does that make sense? I lost weight. I came from a middle-class Jewish family. My father had already died. I had no background or preparation for taking risk. As I said before, my family had no history of investing. My mother really never knew anything about finances. I found that out when my dad died.

Q: I'm laughing about your eight-month bout with trader's flu as you tell me this. I've seen you in action, in the pit. I mean, you're undoubtedly one of the most aggressive traders in the Eurodollar pit.

You stand face to face and take no crap from guys who

are like the monsters of the midway here. You know what I'm saying. Many of the traders you go up against could be professional football or basketball players, and you don't give an inch. It's amazing to watch you in action.

Linda: But you really must understand it took a lot of work. The first eight months I was a total wreck. I had to learn the nature of risk taking and stop thinking of it as gambling. You can say you understand the difference, but you must believe it. I hate gambling. I've never played blackjack. I've never been to Vegas. I don't consider what I do now to be gambling. Other people who don't know the business do. But I don't. Initially it really made me uncomfortable until I could work this issue out in my mind. Getting over that was a big step forward.

Q: So until you worked this out for yourself, the first ten months were really hell?

Linda: Yes, and because I really found it necessary to make the fifty bucks. There were weeks I wouldn't make it, believe it or not.

Q: Did you trade aggressively in the beginning?

Linda: No way.

Q: It is really some contrast to . . .

Linda: My voice was like somebody who had swallowed helium. You know like a little mouse or something. Every time I would bid or offer and a broker would hit me, I found myself saying, Linda, what are you going to do with this? And I really didn't have an answer! As I said before, initially this whole idea of trading was beyond my experience and outside my belief system. Men play poker with the guys. They play gin. Women don't do these things. At least in my family. So initially there was nothing from my training or background that made me feel comfortable about what I was doing.

Q: But yet there must have been something to let you know that you had what it takes, that you could compete and do well.

Linda: Well, eventually, I learned to get confidence in myself. But you see for the first ten months I thought I knew nothing. I said to myself, I don't know anything at all about trading. I don't know anything about the markets. I've never been trained. And I was right. I didn't know anything, but once I gained some knowledge and skills, I had the confidence that I could get, let's say, a B+ and eventually an A.

Q: What were you trading in 1977?

Linda: At first I was trading wheat and silver. I would go back and forth between the two. You see, Bob, I always believed I was book smart. I thought if only I could read up everything there is to know, I would be home free, but that doesn't work in trading. It's not enough to learn about all the right things to do.

Q: Right.

Linda: Then I tried to listen to what everyone told me to do. My ex-husband would say buy this or sell that. Or another guy I knew on the floor would say you've got to buy the soybeans. Which I did and lost.
          This was part of my initial experience, too, listening to what I thought other people knew, assuming unhesitatingly that they were smarter and more knowledgeable than I.

Q: Did they know what they were talking about?

Linda: No! Well, in fairness, they may have, but when you're trading the market, you can't listen to other people's opinions.

Q: You can't rely on them?

Linda: It doesn't work. So you see, the reason I was so uncomfortable, had such a nervous stomach was that I was doing all the wrong things. I had no confidence in myself! I never gave myself a chance to say, hey, Linda, what do you think?

Q: You were doing what everybody else thought was right.

Linda: Yes, I was doing what everyone else thought would make money. Finally, one day I just said to myself, I'm a trader! I know I can do it. I know I can excel at this!

I think it is important that I get across how difficult it was to get to this realization and how much psychological work it took to persist. I think the reason most people don't make it is that they are unwilling to deal with the pain. I can't tell you how many times in the beginning I found myself having to leave the trading floor and cry in the bathroom. I would sit in front of the mirror and say to myself, what am I going to do? I can't do this.

You see, all the commitment and dealing with the pain pays off if you really have the desire to succeed. One day, I remember, I just said, screw this. I'm just going to go in there and do it! No matter what! That's when I started to change.

Q: What did you do that was different?

Linda: I would buy something, and when someone would call me and start giving his trading advice, I would say, don't call me anymore. I didn't care who it was, whether it was my husband at the time or whoever. Don't call me, I'll call you! And I began to listen to myself. I would say from about that time on trading has been like riding a bike. It wasn't like I always did it great, but I began to get the feel for it. Once you learn to ride a bike, you never go back to the stage where you're falling off all the time.

Q: I should point out to the readers that I've seen you on many occasions trade in the pit. You're really amazing. I mean, you're always in the market, always bidding or offering.

Linda: Yes, I'm always in the market.

Q: You're always aggressively in the market. You're always right in there, fighting to get on your trade.

Linda: But that's not hard work. That's different.

Q: How do you maintain that level of motivation? I mean, you go head-to-head with some of the biggest traders on the floor of the exchange.

Linda: You learn, especially being a woman, that you must maintain a certain level of respect. And I just try not to let anyone walk all over me. When I was younger I was much rougher around the edges. It's a lot easier for me now that I can trade at a much higher, let's say, professional level. I've earned my place in the pit, and I get the respect I deserve.

Q: You're in the Eurodollar pit at the CME and before that . . .

Linda: I was at the Mid-America for six years. There are many successful traders who traded there who now trade at the Chicago Board of Trade and the Mercantile Exchange. I believe anyone who was successful at the Mid-Am is usually a good trader.

Q: How long did it take you to become profitable?

Linda: The second year. I started to turn a profit at the end of '78.

Q: And you've been consistently profitable ever since?

Linda: Every year since '78. That year the market in silver turned good, and I've been pretty consistent ever since.

Q: I'd say! I've heard people say and, of course, I don't know if it's true, that you have never had a losing month.

Linda: I've never had a losing week.

Q: Since 1978 you've never had a losing week? I certainly don't want to jinx you. But that's pretty amazing. The other thing that's remarkable is how you stand out on the trading floor. I think in many ways you are probably the only woman on the floor who actually trades such high volume on such a consistent basis with the results that you get.

Linda: It can be very physically tiring. I notice a lot of women, in fact many male traders, who don't have the stamina to work a full day. I'm basically there all day, every day, and I've done it now for almost eighteen years.

Q: How do you psych yourself up each day? How do you maintain that energy level? You just appear so motivated in the pit.

Linda: I've always had a lot of energy, and I just think there's a lot of reasons why I want to succeed. I think everyone has his own reasons for why he does things. I've always been hungry to take care of myself and my family. That's my goal. I'm the kind of person who, once I realize what needs to be done, I go out and do it. I guess once I choose to stop trading, I'll quit and never look back.

Q: Just walk away from it.

Linda: I'll probably just walk away and go on to the next thing. I thought I was going to retire about eight years ago. Remember, I started when I was thirty. I guess it just gets in your blood.

Q: I know, Linda, sometimes you grouse about trading and some of the other traders, but I think what comes through behind the words is you really love it.

Linda: Parts of it I love. And I like it better at some times than at others.

Q: What do you like the most about trading?

Linda: I think the best part is the immediate feedback if you're right or if you're wrong. I really like that.

I like the fact that I don't work for anybody but myself. I'm my own boss. I should also add, nobody could be a tougher boss than me. Nobody.

Q: So you demand a lot of yourself?

Linda: Just terrible. I'm always trying to take it to the next level. If I could just ease up on myself. And that's what I'm really making an effort to do now. That's my current goal. To be a little easier on myself.

Q: Well, that's obviously the key to your success; that you expect so much of yourself and you can deliver. Also, that you can create the internal climate to make it happen. And, yes, you're right, you certainly have earned the right to go easier on Linda Leventhal.

Linda: You really have to know yourself. Everybody can't perform the same way in the same market. I operate best in a steady market. I'm not as good when unemployment figures come out or when there's an element of panic introduced into the market.

Q: You spoke before of expecting a lot of yourself. Could you give me some sense of what that personal standard looks like in terms of your trading?

Linda: This is going to sound funny, but like everyone else, I don't like to lose any money during the day. But, of course, I do. And for the most part, I'm okay with that.

                I think what frustrates me the most or what I get down on myself the most about is if I'm not focused. If I'm not paying attention, if I'm not giving it my all and I make stupid mistakes. It bothers me if I lose money because of that.

Q: Could you talk a little more about your trading focus?

Linda: When you're in the trading pit, I would say it's very much like being in a race or being in a prize fight or for that matter being on the stage. You're performing. You are performing all the time. And if you're not paying full attention, you will get caught. You may have been out too late or maybe you partied too much or whatever. You allow yourself to become distracted. You can lose everything in one momentary lapse. Being focused is really being there.

Q: Linda, when you are focused, what are you looking at?

Linda: I have to look at a lot of things all at once. I have to be aware of all the relevant markets that affect what I'm trading.

For example, right now I'm trading Eurodollars. So I'm definitely watching the bonds. That's what we watch the most. Then I keep track of 5- and 10-year notes. A lot of times I'm also watching the currencies, especially the yen.

I keep in mind the particular relationships between all these things as they are changing day to day and week to week. I let the pattern establish itself, and I go with it. I also watch the S&Ps. Today they've gotten strong, and the bonds started following along. You'll go the same way. The relationships are not always the same. That's why you need the flexibiity to change as the overall patterns are changing.

Q: I think that's what's so hard for other traders to understand—that when someone like you is making that adjustment, it is really intuitive, isn't it?

Linda: Right. It's a constantly changing stream. That's why it's so hard when people read books on trading. They watch the bonds and just focus on that, and they don't realize that it's your intuition about these relationships that you really have to monitor.

One of the things I pay careful attention to is size. I watch how many are bid and offered in the pit at a given price level. To me that's a big issue. For another trader it might not be, but I know how much pressure I might want to take. And even if I may be right in the end, that doesn't often mean anything to me. I want to be right now; otherwise, I'd rather not be in the trade.

Q: So you are looking at how many contracts might be bid or offered in the pit at a particular moment?

Linda: Yes.

Q: How many contracts do you feel comfortable taking at any given trade?

Linda: It depends. Usually not more than a hundred. I feel most comfortable with fifty to seventy-five.

Q: That's the unit you're trading in and out of during the day.

Linda: Yes, usually. In the last five years the volume has gotten so big that most big traders easily take a hundred.

I've had to deal with that issue of size. A couple of years ago I was getting upset; I had to choose whether I wanted to trade huge volume. It was an ego thing with me. It was difficult. I felt that at my age I was trading just the unit that I felt was right. I didn't want to risk anymore than I had to.

Q: You didn't want added exposure?

Linda: Right, I didn't want it. Now I'm comfortable with that. If a broker or someone has a problem with it, then that's their problem.

Q: What does a broker tell you if he tries to give you his whole number and you only take one hundred?

Linda: Well, they don't say anything. They'll just ignore you. And I can understand their point. They may have to get five hundred contracts off or a thousand. They don't want to do just fifty or one hundred. They want two hundred, two hundred, something like that. Often I can be bidding or something way before these other people or maybe someone else can be bidding, and they'll look at him and they'll say, sell you two hundred. And I get nothing.

Q: So they won't respect your first bid if they can't hit you on their whole number.

Linda: Right.

Q: The broker just wants the comfort of getting off his whole number without getting stuck?

Linda: Right. And part of the game is learning how to deal with that.

Q: How many contracts do you usually trade in a given day?

Linda: I would say I trade about five hundred to a thousand.

Q: What's the most you've ever traded in a single day?

Linda: Several thousands.

Q: Linda, when you bid for twenty-five or fifty contracts and you get hit on it, what's the first thing that you think to yourself?

Linda: That's a good question. It depends on who hits you. If it's a broker who never trades with you, you think, where am I going to get out of this?

Q: So that's an important part of the focus also, isn't it? Just knowing who trades with you?

Linda: For sure. I mean, you know, everyone laughs. If so-and-so hits me on a trade, there must be nobody around him who wants it. It's true. But, basically, the key is just stay calm and write the trade down. Even if the market has turned against me in that moment, just stay focused and trust yourself and your game plan.

Q: What happens when the trade immediately goes in your direction? Do you immediately take the profit or do you kind of ride it?

Linda: Almost immediately. Ninety-five percent of the time I take an immediate profit.

Q: You take a one- or two-point profit?

Linda: Yes, it works for me!
               I would say the Eurodollars are different from a lot of pits. Our pit is a slow-moving pit. There is usually quite a bit bid on and quite a bit offered, which makes it a unique kind of trade. And so, when I have the edge, I often take an immediate profit and just keep trying to repeat that process as often as I can.

Q: How many women are there in the Eurodollar pit?

Linda: Right now there are no women brokers in the first option that I can think of, and I think there's one female trader.

Q: That's the option you trade?

Linda: No, I'm in the second option. In my option there are two other women traders.

Q: Would you say there are fewer than ten female traders in the entire Eurodollar pit?

Linda: There are about ten, brokers and traders included; I may be off, it could be more like fifteen. How many traders do you think there are in the entire pit? It's so huge.

Q: Four hundred?

Linda: Oh, at least.

Q: Five hundred?

Linda: I think at least that many. So you can see the percentage of women traders in the pit is pretty small. I think actually the number of female traders has gone down.

Q: You think so? I was about to say I think there are probably more women traders today than ever before.

Linda: Not in the pits.

Q: One thing I do know for sure. You really stand out in that pit. I don't think there's anybody who has the same physical presence that you have, not only in your pit but on the entire trading floor.

Linda: There's no one that's been there as long as I have! Actually, there are some women traders who are very good and probably trade even more than I do in terms of their unit size and overall volume.

Q: What is it like dealing with the guys in the pit? I know from fifteen years of personal experience in the pit that they can be pretty rough.

Linda: There are so many different kinds of men in this business!

Also my initial relationships with men were quite different than they are today.

Q: Of course, you are also married to a trader whom I know very well.

Linda: My husband is nice. He is a nice person in and out of the pit.
        You know, when I started trading, I used to think there were several kinds of male traders. One kind of man was the kind of person who particularly resented women. He resented your being there because his wife was home with the kids. And you were here taking money out of his pocket. This was the kind of guy who thought trading was a closed system. He refused to see that we were all there trying to do the same thing.

Q: Fighting for the same slice of pie.

Linda: Some of these guys, in the early years, really were nasty to me. I was kind of low man on the totem pole.
        The other kind of male trader was the kind of man who, instead of giving me positive suggestions, would speak for me like I didn't have a voice. He would say to the broker, on my behalf, she needs to buy five contracts. She needs to do this, like I'm helpless.

Q: Like he was your guardian. The guardian angel syndrome.

Linda: Yeah. He probably thought he was being nice.

Q: And here you are. You've clearly made your own mark, despite all this. How did you do it? How did you establish your place given the hostile environment?

Linda: I just stood up for myself! To the guy who was trying to be helpful, I finally just said, "Excuse me, I appreciate that, but I can take care of the trading." Really I can. And if I didn't get that trade this time, I'll get the next one.

Q: Where does that confidence come from?

Linda: That's a good question. I don't know. It's funny because

I always thought I didn't have a lot of confidence in myself, but somehow, after that first year of trading experience, I started to build strong confidence in myself.

When I said before I don't think I'm gambling, that's not 100 percent true. What I'm doing as a trader is I'm betting on myself. I'm putting my money on myself that I'm going to know exactly what to do at the right time.

Q: I think you've said that better than anybody I've ever interviewed. That's really the essence of it: your bet is on yourself and your ability, talent, and confidence. Clearly, that's what allows you to be the trader that you are—that you really expect so much of yourself and live up to that expectation.

Linda: Although at times I still think I don't give myself enough credit. I think sometimes it stops me from stepping beyond what I think my boundaries are. For example, I think that if I were younger, I would be a much bigger trader.

Q: Linda, how do you personally overcome a series of losing trades? How do you keep your state of mind high after a series of disappointing trades in the market?

Linda: Well, I just kind of say to myself that this has happened before. It'll happen again. It is a part of a cycle. Fortunately, for me, those losses don't come as often as the winners.

I think often what works for me is walking out of the pit, or even leaving the floor. Leaving the exchange. I get some fresh air, try to get relaxed, and get focused again. I find for me what's key is to not blame yourself when it happens. You must relax and say to yourself, it's okay. You know we can't always be right. It's like playing the TV game "Jeopardy." It seems easy when you're not spinning, when you're sitting on your couch watching it. But when you're in the middle of the pit and everything else is going on, sometimes you just don't react as fast. That's why you get angry at yourself. Oh, I should have reacted faster. I should have bid for it faster; I held back. All this happens in a hundredth of a second. You must relax and take the pressure off yourself and just say you've done it a hundred times before. You're going to come back.

Q: So it's basically a process of refocusing. Mustering up the confidence physically and psychologically that is necessary to get back in there and get back into the fray. To just get into the heart and soul of the trade.

Linda: I just get into a zone.

Q: I think that's really the essence of what you're doing. I mean, other people whom I've interviewed have spoken about "flow" or being lost in time, really being, you know, in a psychological frame of mind where you don't have any consciousness of yourself or time.

Linda: That's me. I really don't.

Q: That's very interesting.

Linda: At times, I think maybe I should. To pay more attention to retracements and what points and . . . . But basically I have no concept of all that when totally focused. I'm just constantly relying on my own intuition about the market.

Q: Where you feel it's right to buy and where it's right to sell?

Linda: If I had to rely on just one thing in my trading, it would be my intuition. If I didn't get to look at where the bonds were, if I didn't see what the brokers were bidding on, it would be just that gut feeling that I get of when to get into the market and when to get out.

Q: Linda, could you describe specifically how you use your intuition?

Linda: For example, some days I'll keep trying to buy the market. I'll be trading in and out from the long side. In other words, I keep looking to buy the market on a break or retracement. All of a sudden, I'll get a feeling and I'll say to myself, this market feels heavy. That's exactly what I'll say, it feels heavy; meaning it doesn't feel right. I think it's going up. But if I rely on my intuition, my intuition tells me it feels heavy.

Q: And your intuition ... I mean, you're pointing to your stomach.

Linda: Yeah.

Q: Your intuition is signaling sell when your mind is telling you to buy ... and you go with the feeling?

Linda: I'm saying it's more than just a feeling, it's vital information. If my head says buy and I keep trying to buy and it isn't working, and all of a sudden my stomach tells me it feels heavy, I will rely on my intuition. I'm going with my stomach! Most times I won't be able to even verbalize it. It just happens automatically. Experience has taught me to trust it.

Q: I think that's very typical that people don't verbalize it. The interesting thing is, and I want to get your take on this, I think the most successful traders have the capability to rely on intuitive information and act on it in the way that you described, automatically, without second-guessing themselves.

Linda: I think that is true. I think the best traders are listening to their gut feelings a lot more than other traders.

Q: Can you think of a specific example of a trade that you were in recently where relying on your intuition proved to be successful?

Linda: Just the other day something happened that happens a lot of times and my intuition saved me a bundle. The market, you could feel, was about to go sellers. You could just feel it, but it was my intuition that told me don't sell it, buy it! I felt it was a trap. Sure enough the market went eight sellers, nine bids.

Q: What happened?

Linda: My intuition was right. It was a trap. The momentum of the market was to the short side, but my sense, my intuition based on my trading experience, was if you sell it you will get caught. It was just that sense of it that kept me from following the break.

Q: The feeling?

Linda: Yes, that's why I didn't sell them. In fact, as I said, I bought them and I made money selling them in time. But, again, the only reason I did that was because my intuition informed me that it was a trap.

Q: How many times a day do you get those feelings?

Linda: If you're talking about pure intuition, maybe once a day ... maybe more. The point I really want to make is that when I get that feeling of pure intuition, I can rely on it implicitly.

Q: Linda, what do you think are the characteristics of successful traders? What common traits do you think set them apart?

Linda: I think they have an enormous amount of confidence in themselves. They also have to have a strategy or a set of rules or strategy. They don't have to verbalize it, but they need something that they can follow when they trade. They need discipline. They have to know when to and when not to trade.

Q: How do you determine when it is a good time to trade and when it's not a good time to trade?

Linda: Intuition. My stomach usually tells me when not to trade. When the market doesn't follow any of the normal things that I rely on. It gets choppy or thin, and it starts going around from one place to another without rhyme or reason. I start to feel that if I get into the trade that I won't know when to get out. The point is that I feel all this in an instant without having to think about it. That's my discipline. That's how I can keep control.

Q: That's an interesting idea. Following your intuition gives a feeling of greater control. Is that it?

Linda: Right. I'm not saying I couldn't make a lot of money or lose a lot of money trading in a choppy market, but it won't feel right. I can feel it in my stomach. I'm real anxious about trading at those times. I'm not comfortable about it. I try only to trade when I can feel relaxed without those anxieties, when I feel I'm in control.

Q: So, I guess that would be another characteristic of successful traders from your point of view, having control over your methodology.

Linda: Of course. A couple of weeks ago Greenspan was talking in the afternoon. Nobody expected him to be talking at that time, and the market started acting really silly running up and then breaking off for no apparent reason. There were several times when brokers tried to get me into positions. You know, they tried to dump a hundred contracts on me here or there, and I just refused to take them.

Q: Just move their order.

Linda: Yes, just because my badge was in front of their face.

Now in a normal market, if I only wanted to buy or sell fifty, and a broker gave me a hundred, I might do it, as a scratch; that's fine with me. I don't care about the commission. But in this kind of market, it was flying around ten points at a time. I just said, "No way, I'm sorry."

The funny thing is this trade they wanted me to take, of course, went my way. It would have made five thousand dollars in a matter of seconds. But, you see, it was just luck. It could have also gone the other way.

Q: I think what you're saying is that you have a set of rules which governs your trading at all times and along with your intuition comprises your trading strategy.

Linda: Right.

Q: And you don't break those rules?

Linda: No . . . well, I do on occasion, but I try not to.

Q: So is the focus coming in every day and trying to stick to those rules, to your trading strategy, even though you might have the temptation to go outside of them or take the extra shot?

Linda: Yes, I religiously try and stick by them, but again, sometimes I break those rules. That's when I get on myself.

Q: Do you think if you would open up more and rely on your intuitive sense to even a greater degree it would be helpful?

Linda: Yes.

Q: To know when you can violate your trading rules?

Linda: Exactly. To know that even though my rules tell me not to take more than one hundred, there are times when . . .

Q: I think it's important to state for the young traders that this intuition grows out of the veteran experience of years of trading. I mean we wouldn't want a young trader to start violating his own rules. But I think someone who has been around and who does have a very strong intuitive sense that has been battle-tested in the market knows when doing just that is appropriate.

Linda: Absolutely. I know in the markets when I can absolutely violate some of the rules as far as trading bigger and when I shouldn't. That again is where trusting your intuition comes in.

Q: Someone once said there are only two rules in trading: Rule number one is never violate your trading rules, rule number two is know when to violate rule number one.

Linda: That's a cute way of putting it. It is true, though. There are times when they can be violated, definitely. But, of course, you need the experience and the intuition to keep you out of trouble.

Q: We were talking about characteristics of successful traders. What about independence of mind, having your own point of view about the market? It seems that was one of the things that initially helped you to become success-ful—realizing that you didn't have to listen to what other traders had to say, that you had to rely on your own judgment and intuition.

Linda: I just have confidence to trust my own thoughts and feelings.

Q: I think it is just that level of confidence which gives you the independence of mind to rely on your intuition and not necessarily know where the next move in the market is, but to know when it happens you will be there.

Linda, how important do you think optimism is as far as trading goes?

Linda: Very.

Q: Could you talk a little bit about that?

Linda: I just know that I try and come in every day, every morning, no matter what happened the day before, with the outlook that today's a new day. I say hello to everybody who's standing around me, ask them if they had a nice evening, and just keep a strong and positive mental outlook. Having positive feelings about your trading really helps. I notice that when I come in grumpy, when I'm upset with something someone did or someone said the day before, my trading is off.

Q: You said earlier when you have a string of losses you walk out of the pit. What do you say to yourself to calm down and elevate your state?

Linda: I just say to myself that I have to be strong and confident and positive to trade well. So I tell myself to calm down and get on with it.

Q: You know the thing that comes through to me in this interview is how much you really love to trade.

Linda: I guess that's true. A few years ago I don't know that I would have said that.

Q: I mean, you talk about your trading with such animation.

A lot of thought has obviously gone into your trading. I know we all grump about the frustrations of the floor, but you know, if you could study your body language as I'm studying it as we're talking, I think it would be clear to you how much you love trading.

Linda: For an observer, you're doing a good job.

Q: Thanks. I do want to ask you about something else. Having a husband who is a trader, what are dinnertime conversations like at your home?

Linda: We don't talk about trading at home.

Q: You don't talk about trading at all?

Linda: Paul would probably like to talk about it more than I would.

Q: He never tells you he has a good trade for you?

Linda: No.

Q: Do you ever tell him you have a good trade for him?

Linda: No! No! No! But I know Paul likes to brag about me. I work so hard at work that when I leave, I truly like to put it behind me.

I like to leave the emotion of it behind. I like to cook dinner or take a walk or do other things. I think that keeps me fresh and allows me to be intuitive.

Q: Are you as competitive in other things as you are in trading?

Linda: That's interesting. No, I don't think so. I know I am very competitive; I think I'm less competitive, though, against other people. I think it's more of a competition with myself.

Q: Who's winning?

Linda: That's a good question. I guess I would say if I know I can't win, then I don't want to play.

Q: It's obvious you have chosen an arena where you win with remarkable consistency. Any final words of advice?

Linda: I would just say have a game plan in mind. Have goals that are realistic goals for you. Analyze those goals every week. Notice how you've done following the rules that you've set for yourself and stay within that discipline. Keep a positive attitude. You will experience pain, but you will grow from overcoming your fears and being in control. Definitely be prepared to work hard. People think, in this business, if they can go in and work for half an hour a day and make a couple of trades, then they can go out for the rest of the day. Be successful in trading and then, only then, can you choose to do that!

Q: I always say to people: Be prepared to work harder at this than anything else you ever worked at in your entire life and then, maybe, you'll do well.

Linda: The psychological demands sometimes seem endless. You really need to put your mind in it.

Q: But it still is the ultimate trip, isn't it?

Linda: It is. I started almost twenty years ago, and I thought this is a great job. Flexible hours. Come and go when you want. I don't think I've ever left work early!

Chapter Nine

Howard Abell

Howard Abell is the chief operating officer of Innergame Partners, a firm conducting proprietary trading. He was a long-term member of the Chicago Mercantile Exchange. Formerly, he was president of Abell Asset Management Corp., a Commodity Trading Advisor; and C.S.A., Inc., a futures commission merchant. He is coauthor of The Innergame of Trading *(Irwin, 1993),* The Outer Game of Trading *(Irwin, 1994), and* The Insider's Edge *(Probus, 1985).*

Q: Howard, could you begin by saying something about how you first got started in trading?

Howard: My interest in trading began a very long time ago. I was a stockbroker in New York and did commodity business as well. In those days, commodities was seen only as an adjunct to a stockbroker's normal business. But gradually my attention was drawn to the commodity business. I found it more rewarding and deeply challenging. Eventually I developed a business exclusively in the agricultural commodities area.

Q: What year was that?

Howard: 1968.

Q: How would you characterize those early years and the nature of the business that you were doing? And could you also speak about the training and preparation that you had to go through before you actually started to trade for your own account?

Howard: I was very fortunate. In those years the training available on Wall Street was tremendous. The firm where I was working, Bache and Company, had a training program for their account executives that lasted seventeen weeks. It was an intensive 9-to-5, five-day-a-week school that concentrated on finance, banking, accounting, and sales. The courses were taught at the college level and provided a very fine and comprehensive overview of the financial industry. It was my first serious look at the world of trading.

Q: What was it during the early period that really attracted you to trading?

Howard: From the very beginning I was drawn to trading. You know how you are naturally drawn to certain things. That's how trading was for me. From the start I liked it. I liked the challenge of it. I liked the opportunity to have success over a very short period of time. And I liked the constant movement, the dynamic nature of being part of the market. Naturally, it was truly a fascination and challenge. You might even say an infatuation with the excitement and intellectual challenge of trading.

Q: Have those qualities remained constant? Do you feel that same excitement today?

Howard: Yes. Absolutely.

Q: As much as you did before?

Howard: Perhaps even more today! The challenge is constant. There is so much to learn. It is like the story of Louis Agassiz and the fish. Louis Agassiz was a well-known Harvard biology professor. He once asked one of his most promising students to study a recently caught fish. Again and again the student would return to his mentor and report his observations about the fish: its texture, color, chemical composition, habitat, etc. But, with every new detail of information offered by the student, Dr. Agassiz remarked, "You still have not grasped the essence of the fish."

Finally one day the student returned to the laboratory and, with a heightened sense of understanding, observed, "I'll never truly understand this fish." To this, Louis Agassiz beamed a tremendous smile and said, "Yes, what you have learned is the beginning of true understanding!"

You can never truly learn everything about yourself or the markets. It's a never-ending journey of finding out and exploiting your intellectual curiosity and testing your perceptions. There is the ongoing experience of self-discovery.

Q: You left Wall Street and you became a member of the Chicago Board of Trade. Is that correct?

Howard: Yes. From Wall Street I came to La Salle Street. At first, I became a member of the Chicago Board of Trade and then later a member of the Chicago Mercantile Exchange, where I concentrated in livestock futures and, after they were introduced, in the financial markets.

Q: Initially, what was your early trading experience like?

Howard: It was a very exciting time. The markets were young. There was a lot going on in that period. The grain and livestock markets were very dynamic with volatile price swings. These were historic markets. It was also a time when world-shaking events dictated market movement in very dramatic ways. There was the war in Vietnam, Nixon's resignation, and instability with the Russians. These external events fueled our markets, so that anyone who was actively participating felt he was truly at the center of the universe.

I can remember specifically the 1973 grain market. There was talk of an impending summit meeting with the Russians. There was also the general perception that the Soviets had a severe need for foodstuffs. And there were reports that their harvest was not going well. But because of the nature of their society, we weren't getting much in the way of accurate information.

The grains were slowly starting to move higher. But at first there was nothing extraordinary about it. Then we bombed Hai Phong Harbor. The consensus on La Salle Street was that the bombing would absolutely destroy any chance of the summit meeting with the Russians taking place. But within a day or two, it was very apparent that not only was the summit meeting not called off, but there was intense interest in making sure that it continued despite the bombing. That's when intuition suggested the enormous need for the Soviets to buy our grains. A truly significant market was developing. In fact, what occurred over the next nine months was an historic rally in all the grain markets.

Q: Were you able to capitalize on that intuition?

Howard: Absolutely. I mean, there was a two-dollar rally in the wheat. This was a very significant price movement. It doesn't happen very often. The experience gave me some real insight into the opportunities and success available to you if you have the ability to follow strong convictions. It was also the first time I began to look at the market as something more than an objective road map. In the psychological sense, the map is not the territory.

Q: Howard, is it fair to say you were an instant success?

Howard: No. At the time of this historic grain market that I described, I had been following markets throughout most of the 1960s and early 1970s. This "overnight success" was the culmination of a lot of experience and study.

Hard work is an essential ingredient of success. You cannot approach trading in a half-ass way. It requires total commitment to what you're doing, a belief in your ability to do it, and constant monitoring of yourself and the marketplace for ideas and opportunities.

Q: You've had a very successful career as a floor trader, first at the Board of Trade and then later at the CME. At some point, however, you decided you wanted to trade up-stairs in front of a screen. Can you describe what the transition was like?

Howard: There is a huge difference between floor trading and screen trading. The markets are the same and the concepts of successful trading are all the same. But I think what people who trade on the floor of the exchange face when they come off the floor is the absence of sensory information that they normally receive and can rely on on the floor of the exchange ... the sight of traders bidding and offering and the pervasive noise of open outcry.

Q: The intensity of sound?

Howard: The intensity of sound and the absence of sound. These are tremendous clues for most successful pit traders. And the sights and sounds, more importantly, lead to your feelings, just as the stark reactions that you have to the market do. Price and value are something you see both on the floor and off the floor. However, when you're sitting in an office and watching a screen, you are missing the additional physical clues that you needed as a local.

Q: So how did you adjust?

Howard: It's a very interesting question and the process itself is interesting also. You take your experiences from the past, and you try to relate them to what you see on the screen. In my case, I rely on my intuition. As the market moves and I watch the screen, I monitor my own feeling and mental images. With each price movement, I can see and hear and feel what's going on as if I were still on the floor. I can literally hear the sound of the ticks being made on that screen. I can visualize brokers bidding and offering on the price. I am constantly creating in my own mind the scenario of what's happening on the floor. Based on all those sights and sounds and intuitions, if you will, I decide where to enter or exit the market.

A climax in a fast market provides a very simple way to illustrate this point. Many people without any floor experience can get very excited just watching the screen at these times without actually seeing or hearing the commotion that's taking place on the trading floor. When you're sitting in front of a screen, if you think about it, you can see and feel the climax that takes place, which is to say, the sudden cessation of emotionality in the market. You can "feel" that the market is at a turning point.

Q: Did you encounter any problems in the transition to becoming an upstairs trader?

Howard: Yes. I have a natural tendency to see many market opportunities. When I was on the floor I tended to trade fewer markets. When I began sitting in front of a screen, it took me a while to develop the level of focus I had on the floor. I was always tempted to trade many different markets at once and that can be very debilitating.

Q: There is a very prevalent perception that floor traders have an edge on all other traders. Personally I think it is pure illusion. I'm wondering what is your opinion on this question, and do you think the opportunities are greater on or off the floor, considering you have been successful in both arenas?

Howard: Well, if somebody upstairs in front of a screen tries to do a scalper's job on the floor of the exchange, he is not going to be successful. On the other hand, if a scalper tries to do a trader's job, he's not going to be successful either. What we're really talking about is focus. The trader who is focusing on very small price increments and wants to capitalize on them has a distinct advantage in being in the pit. The trader who is focusing on taking wider price movements in the market can execute his trading strategy anywhere without disadvantage. It comes down to identifying market opportunities through your particular focus and executing decisively.

Q: I've heard you say many times when you are working with novice traders that it's really important that they know what kind of trader they are. Could you elaborate on that?

Howard: I think the point that I try to make is that most beginnng traders get into trouble as a result of starting out with one methodology and then changing in midstream to another, thereby screwing up their performance. You cannot enter into a trade as a day trade and then turn it into a position trade because there's a loss on the trade. The internal logic of the trade must stay consistent. You must know if you're a scalper, day trader, position trader, or spreader and then stick to that methodology.

Q: Of course, on the trading floor one often hears of scalpers who get caught turning into position traders.

Howard: Exactly. The losing scalp turns into a position trade.

Q: What are your current goals?

Howard: In the last ten years I have essentially traded from upstairs. This experience has shaped my trading methodology and goals. My current goal is to become even more effective in terms of executing my trading strategies. With the technology that is available today, with the right structure and in the right circumstances, you can essentially become a floor trader off the floor of the exchange. Not a pit trader, not a scalper, but somebody who is trying to sense the market from day to day and take advantage of those opportunities, as well as catching the longer and deeper trends. I know this may sound contradictory to what I was saying earlier—that you have to know exactly what kind of trader you are. However, I think personally my trading experience is such that I can formulate strategies to capture both short- and long-term moves.

Q: Have you developed this strategy to manage the volatility?

Howard: Yes. To manage the volatility and to take advantage of it in the same way that a floor trader would. Not a scalper, but a floor trader who is looking to exploit a larger piece of a day or two-day market move.

Q: How did you develop your current trading method and what is the basis for your buying and selling decisions?

Howard: I think the most accurate answer to your question is that my current trading method is based on all my past trading experience. Most importantly, what I know intuitively has been successful for me over the years. I want to be a trend player, but not get fixed on the idea of the entire trend in any one particular market. I tend to use very simple chart techniques to allow me to trade with the trend in order to catch near-term moves. The charting techniques that I use derive from classical chart analysis. It works for me for two reasons. First, I am very comfortable with its use. It allows me to make quick judgments that I can readily act on. And, second, it's simplicity itself. I think most traders can be successful using a simple method. It doesn't mean it's easy, but it's simple. When people try to make the simple complex, their trading suffers. They start suffering from anxiety, hesitation, and insecurity. To be an effective trader, you have to be able to react to the trade without any emotional content. I also think when your system has too much complexity, you are always second-guessing and finding yourself having to deal with contradictory indicators.

Q: Howard, could you talk about your interest in and involvement with the psychology of trading? When did it first come to your attention that there was a serious link between psychology and trading performance?

Howard: That notion came to me over a long period of time. I would have the opportunity to observe many traders and see how their attitudes and beliefs about the market and themselves influenced their trading.

Q: In your opinion, what are the ingredients of successful trading?

Howard: You go onto the trading floor and you see there is such a variety of techniques, strategies, and approaches for trading markets successfully. There are some traders who trade every day on the floor of the exchange and will tell you that they rarely have a losing day. And for some, that may even be true! However, if you analyzed their results, as I have, you would see their results are not that impressive considering the opportunities that exist. There are others that tell you that they have wide volatility and, yet, they're making enormous sums of money. So you must find your own approach. You must develop the intuition to trust your own judgments about the market without hesitation or qualification. I strongly believe the key factor for success in trading, as with everything else, is knowing yourself.

Q: Drawing from some of the top traders that you have known personally or who have traded through your clearing firm, what would you say are the other key qualities of successful trading?

Howard: I think most people who come to trading and are not successful come to it either on a lark or see it as a fast path to easy money. Nothing could be further from the truth. Trading is very, very difficult! And the reason it's difficult is because you're up against the most sophisticated people in the world. Yes, of course, there are tremendous opportunities and that's what attracts them. But you must understand who you are competing against in addition to always being in a contest with yourself. There has to be a tremendous commitment to work and a commitment to yourself to do whatever it takes emotionally to play in this very professional arena. It's the major leagues.

Q: Why do you think success is so elusive for most traders? Why do most traders have such a difficult time at it?

Howard: I think it all has to do with your emotional makeup and personal belief system. People who have difficulty being successful at trading are only reinforcing what they believe about themselves through trading. It's the ultimate psychological report card.

Q: Could you talk about that in more personal terms? Could you identify some belief within you that you found it necessary to change?

Howard: Sure. I think this same thing occurs to most traders. One of the most difficult decisions to make as a trader is to either buy or sell the market when it appears like everybody else is doing the opposite—which is to say, in practical terms, buying low and selling high is a very difficult thing to do. The reason that it is so difficult is that you are going against what is perceived to be the "right direction." In point of fact, exploiting these opportunities is the only way you're ever going to be able to buy the low end of a market and sell the high end of a market.

The traders that come to the marketplace with the conviction and proven methodology to sell when everyone wants to buy and to buy when everyone wants to sell are, in my opinion, the most successful traders.

In personal terms, developing this belief system early on was difficult for me. When I felt weakness and perceived a breaking market, I had a tendency to sell into the weakness. In other words, when I first started trading, my focus was only on one side of the market. I would neglect thinking about where this market was going to stop, and consequently, I would miss the turning point and find myself chasing the market back up. These are subtleties that we are talking about: having these insights and being able to distinguish between the times you should sell weakness and when you should fade the weakness comes from years of market experience and intuition.

To be successful in trading, you must constantly construct new patterns of behavior that will assure effective action. You have to look at both your successes and failures critically under a microscope with objectivity to determine what you are doing right and what you are doing wrong. You modify your methodology and your attitudes about trading until you can come up with a formula that works consistently.

As I said before, I had to learn how to separate my own opinion of the market with an objective point of view. Once I learned how to do this, I could create a strategy for buying low and selling high. The axioms work. The challenge is to figure out a way that they work for you.

Q: Howard, let's focus for a second on loss, a much-neglected topic in trading books. As you know, for most traders this is not a particularly theoretical experience. In fact, attitudes about loss and losing will predict trading outcomes. I know today taking losses doesn't bother you at all in terms of maintaining your focus. But early on in your career did it bother you to take losses?

Howard: It never really did. Let me just qualify that by saying I was more fearful of larger losses, so I understood the money management concepts of taking small losses. Many traders fear giving away built-up profit. I never had that trouble. I gave away a lot of profit. Seriously, I always had the ability to stay with the good trade and ride it until the market proved me wrong.

Q: I hesitate to mention this. You and I have this long-standing joke that when you're in a winning position, there's really nobody better than you in riding it all the way to the end. I always say to you that you and Warren Buffet share something in common: Both of you wake up each morning and say, "Where do I take profit?"

Howard: That's a good problem to have. It's a very interesting issue, I think, after dealing with the question of loss. The second most difficult thing for traders to do is learn how not to take immediate profit. For many traders this is much more debilitating on a psychological level than taking a loss.

Maximizing the profit is key. When a profit presents itself, if you take it right away, you're reducing your opportunity to make up for all those small losses that are essential in the trading process. Remember, the nature of this business is that it is difficult to be able to be right more times than wrong. Therefore, if you don't maximize your profits, you are always playing catch up.

Q: Howard, did it take you a long time to be able to develop that ability to go for the long pull rather than get caught up in the momentary emotion of the immediate profit?

Howard: I had a very good teacher, George Segal. He is probably the best trader I have ever seen who could trade like this in a very large way. In the 1970s and 1980s, the two of us were significant players in the livestock markets on the Chicago Mercantile Exchange and in the grains to a smaller extent. When opportunity presented itself, if you had the fortitude to stay with the trend, the rewards were considerable. Getting into the trend and then staying with it required conviction, patience, and equity. Watching George execute these strategies successfully was a tremendous learning experience for me.

Q: Speaking of George, I've heard you say many times that he's probably the greatest intuitive trader that you've ever known. I've heard you tell stories about how George could be in a position for months and just get a flash or have a dream that would make him immediately sell out a huge position. What was it about George's trading that allowed him to rely so unswervingly on his intuition?

Howard: Early on in my career when I first came to Chicago, an old timer at the Chicago Board of Trade said to me the best traders rely solely on their intuition. It is their gift. That is George's gift. In my view, after twenty-five years of trading, I believe intuition is the sum total of all the stimuli that traders receive in an instant or over time and also the sum total of all their experiences in the market.

Q: And the ability to process that information?

Howard: Yes, and the ability to process that. Subconsciously, your mind is helping you to make decisions based on all the stimuli that you really can't consciously process. As an example, George would be able to stay in a position for a very long period of time, weeks and weeks, and then just one day come in and for no apparent or objective reason say, "Sell out."

Q: Out of the blue.

Howard: Oh, he would say he couldn't sleep or just had a funny feeling. And more often than not, he was absolutely correct. Did he catch every high and low? Obviously not. But that is not really the essential point. The essential point is knowing when to get out of a good position as well as a bad one. They haven't yet invented a market indicator that comes close to George's intuition.

Q: Howard, what else did you learn from George about intuitive trading?

Howard: George was and is probably one of the top livestock fundamentalists in the country. And since he is someone who looks at the fundamental aspects of the market, you tend to overlook his intuitive strengths. I think his success comes from an ability to translate his fundamental knowledge into what the market says to him, and he trusts what he sees, hears, and feels. So that if he observed the technicals at any particular time were changing and a trend was developing in the market, he would first wait for the market to tell him. Which meant that he would rely on his own intuition.

They say timing is everything. And George's intuition gives him the ability to wait for the fundamentals to show themselves in the market. And then he enters the market. But it is not fundamentals or technicals that get him in, it is the ability to trust his judgment and make a commitment to that market in a way that is substantial.

Q: Howard, you've known many great traders over the years, some who were mechanical traders and others who were discretionary traders. In your view, who are the very best traders?

Howard: That's a difficult question. I believe that every type of trader, whether systems or discretionary, can be successful. I think that the most consistently profitable traders are the ones who can rely on their intuition as a trading tool.

In my experience, the most successful traders take all the information that is available to them and are not afraid to make the judgments and decisions based on their intuition in a very decisive and significant way. I think when a trader has that level of conviction and commitment to his own abilities, he will have the confidence level, and of course I'm assuming competence, to commit to his market. People who use computerized systems tend to do it in a very mechanical way. Their reliance is more on the machinery than the creativity, if you will, of the trade.

Q: Why do you think it is so difficult for most traders to trust their intuition?

Howard: I think it is a self-trust issue. It's a self-esteem issue. Traders are always asking themselves if they can really trust a feeling. I know the answer has to be "yes."

Q: Of course, you wouldn't want somebody to trust his feelings if he had only been trading for a short period of time.

Howard: Of course. This comes with experience, a great deal of experience.

Q: Howard, can you think of an example of a trader you've worked with on an individual basis whose intuition you helped develop? And how did you do it?

Howard: In many of the seminars and personal consultations that I've done, I've emphasized the importance of learning to trust your intuition. What I do and what I have done in the past is learn the system that is being used and then critically evaluate if there is proven reliability to the method in a statistical sense. If I am convinced there is validity to the approach, I then try to get the trader to believe in himself and the method he is employing—to make him believe that it works.

For example, if you draw a simple trend line on a chart, most traders will readily agree that trading at or against the trendline works many more times than not. In fact, even if it doesn't work, it gives you a great deal of valuable information with which you can proceed in the market. The point is, if the line is held, you can buy against the trend line. You can identify your risk, which will be relatively small at any given time. You have, in short, a system that identifies points of entry and exit with defined risk and acceptable reliability. The challenge, of course, is to condition yourself to routinely act with conviction and decision at the point of opportunity. The intuition will grow from the discipline and experience of executing the system.

Q: Are you saying that the intuition comes from having the commitment and the conviction to take every trade within your system, within the parameters that you set for yourself?

Howard: Exactly. What you believe about your system!

Q: Doesn't it really all come down to what you believe about yourself?

Howard: Our beliefs are the lenses through which we see the world. What you believe about yourself and the market will ultimately predict your performance. One of the exercises that I do with my traders illustrates this point.

Q: Tell me about it.

Howard: I bring a group of four or five traders into a large room. I scatter a half dozen chairs so that they look like obstacles between the entrance of the room and the window at the far end. I then tell them to fix in their minds exactly where each chair is placed, because in a moment I will ask them to navigate their way across the room blindfolded. In the meantime I remove all the chairs so that there is in actuality a clear path. There are no impediments at all.

It's incredibly interesting to see how each trader attempts to overcome this challenge. Some are unbelievably hesitant, others lurch forward, throwing all caution to the wind.

When the traders reach the other side, I take off the blindfolds. Often they look at me with amazement and intuitively understand the point of the exercise. In their mind, they were seeing chairs where there were none. We all operate in the markets with a set of beliefs that either enhance or inhibit our trading performance. We furnish the living rooms of our own minds!

Q: Howard, are there any other ways to help traders develop their intuition as traders?

Howard: Yes. Traders truly have to understand exactly how they are reacting both physically and mentally to the market-place. They have to understand their own feelings and the emotional process that is taking place when they're taking losses or profits or deciding, sometimes in anguish, whether or not to take a trade.

Traders need to look at what makes the successes successful—and very objectively attempt to make themselves operate in the successful mode all the time or as much of the time as possible. It requires a great deal of introspection and looking at yourself and the trading process under a microscope.

Q: It sounds like an adventure in self-discovery.

Howard: Absolutely. Trading is self-discovery. You can tell who you are and what you are by how you trade.

The reward of all this self-analysis is the ability to use what we call intuition. Without the work—without the commitment to put in the time and look at how you are internalizing market events—there will be no strong and reliable intuition in the end.

Q: So, Howard, in your view, the first step is the commitment to developing the mechanical skills of trading?

Howard: Yes.

Q: And knowing also that ultimately you have to rely on yourself alone?

Howard: Yes. Knowing that you have to ultimately rely only on yourself. And also coming to the absolute belief and confidence that your market approach and your proven trading abilities are all you really need.

Q: You know, it sounds like such a simple concept. But we've known many traders over the years . . . this idea of taking personal responsibility for your own actions and relying on yourself, as obvious as it sounds, it's not that easy for traders.

Howard: Yes, that's absolutely true! We use language that tells us that. We blame the market. We say, "The market got me." We blame the broker or the fill. The fill is always the worst when we're taking a loss. Of course, it is never as bad when we're taking a profit.

We say that we take a loss. We make them, we create the losses. And in that creation we have to learn how to create very small ones instead of very big ones. I think taking personal responsibility, assuming it intuitively, is an essential key to trading success.

Q: Howard, you've traded now for over twenty-five years. I know how much you still love the whole enterprise of trading markets. Can you talk about the importance of your enthusiasm for trading and how that relates to trading performance?

Howard: It always amazes me to find people who want to trade who really do not enjoy, dare I say love, the process. They literally agonize over every potential loss or anguish over the process of making a decision about taking a profit. Essentially, they're always in agony. You must love this process passionately to be successful. The passion is what allows you to step up to every challenge.

It also has to be fun, not in the sense of a laugh a minute but in the sense of enjoying the process. The intuition grows from the enjoyment of it and the sense of fulfillment that you derive from trading.

I believe intuition is not possible without the enjoyment and the sense of fulfillment. People become intuitive about what they're doing when they're really fully immersed in it.

Q: So, Howard, in a personal sense, trading still provides you with the same excitement and enjoyment that it did in the very beginning.

Howard: Just as much.

Chapter Ten

Tom Belsanti

Tom Belsanti is an independent trader and member of the International Monetary Market Division of the Chicago Mercantile Exchange. He is a former partner and executive council member of Skylane Trading Group. He has extensive experience trading a variety of futures products, including interest rates, stock options, foreign currencies, grains, and livestock.

Q: Tom, how did you get started in trading?

Tom: I was working as a clerk for a very large order filler in the Eurodollar pit.

     For a long time the Eurodollar contract was very slow. Then, around 1983 business got progressively busier. The volume picked up enormously and the clearing houses started trading a lot more size. I was a good clerk and had the respect of the customers. The broker I was working for offered me the opportunity to get a trading badge so I could help him handle all the business. He provided the guarantee for my seat and helped me open up a trading account.

Q: Were you mostly trading or filling paper at first?

Tom: From 1983 to 1987 I was primarily a broker handling customer orders.

Q: When did you make the transition from broker to trader?

Tom: As I said, in 1987, just about a month before the stock crash. Business was so wild. Business was booming, and I couldn't have been happier with the amount of brokerage I was handling, but it was also a time when any errors were passed on to the brokers.

I ate my errors. I ate my clerk's errors. I ate the phoneman's errors. I was even eating errors from the customers! One day I finally decided that I would much rather trade on my own and have responsibility for my actions alone, win or lose. I've always been willing to pay for my own errors. It's handling everybody else's mistakes that made me go nuts!

Q: What was the biggest error you ever had to eat?

Tom: I had to eat a thirty-two thousand dollar customer error!

Q: That couldn't have tasted very good.

Tom: No. Well, if it had been mine, it might have tasted better, but it was someone else's error.

Q: Basically, at this point you just said to yourself, this is a lot of crap and there must be an easier way?

Tom: I was determined to start trading my own money and, as I said, just be responsible for my own errors.

Q: What made you think that you had what it takes to be a trader?

Tom: Since I was the secondary broker, there were many times during the day where I found myself standing around basically doing nothing. I began to seriously watch the market and develop a sense of what moved it.

I knew what to do as a broker, but I really didn't know what the locals were doing. So the times that I stood around, without any orders to fill, I began to pay very close attention to the floor traders: watching them bid and offer and move size. At a certain point it occurred to me that it's a lot easier to be a floor trader than a broker. At least I thought it would be easier.

Q: Tom, do you think that experience of four or five years as a broker was good training to become a trader?

Tom: I absolutely believe it has made me a better local. When I made the transition, I had mastered most of the basic skills, writing down trades, flipping my cards, and remembering trades. My counting capabilities were just enhanced by all the experience of handling paper.

Q: You're talking about mechanical skill?

Tom: Yes, just all the considerable mechanical skills that you need to perfect that most people don't even think about. As you know, it takes years for some floor traders just to perfect their arsenal of purely mechanical skills.

Q: What about the actual decision making of trading? You know, knowing when to buy and when to sell?

Tom: In the beginning I was under the false impression that as a local all my decisions to buy and sell would be dictated by my ability to capture the edge. You see, when I was an order filler I would repeatedly watch the customers complain about selling the bid, but I would also see the local smile when he bought the bid. So I thought that all you had to do was just work for the edge: buy the bid and sell the offer. It takes a long time before one broadens one's perspective about trading and sees that there is a lot more to it than capturing a simple edge. You do want an edge, of course, but it is never just as simple as my first impression of trading was.

Q: Did the other locals accept you right away as a trader?

Tom: Pretty much. Of course, at the time there were many traders who were much larger than I, so my volume posed no threat. Then, in 1989, when business surged in the pit, where you stood became very important. You literally had to stake out and fight for your piece of real estate.

Q: Tom, today you can and often do trade a thousand contracts in one shot. Give me some sense of what the progression was like from being a novice trader to becoming a seasoned veteran.

Tom: I think with trading you have to view everything that you do as a learning experience. That has always been my attitude. I love to trade, and I'm there to learn. That is my commitment. The numbers grow naturally as you develop new skills and techniques.

Q: Did success come to you right away?

Tom: You must have your own definition of success. Initially, my goal was to make thirty to fifty ticks a day (each tick in the Eurodollar pit is $25). After I achieved my goal I would play defense or trade only when I could get into the market on the bid or offer. ·

Q: What size were you trading at this time?

Tom: Ten to twenty, never more than fifty. If a broker hit me on fifty, I was looking to immediately hit the locals next to me. I was basically a ten- to twenty-lot trader, and I felt I could make two to three good twenty-lot trades a day. That's why my goal was set at fifty ticks a day.

Q: How did you move from being a twenty-lot trader to trading the size you trade today?

Tom: After the stock crash, the volatility in the market was unbelievable. Brokers needed to move their paper fast and wanted nothing to do with a ten- or twenty-lot trader. I just naturally started to trade fifty. Just getting the taste of making two or three ticks on a fifty-lot or a hundred-lot broadened my goal to making three to four times what I thought I could make earlier.

Q: What are your trading goals currently?

Tom: That's a really interesting question. You see at first, in my early years of trading, my trading goals were always monetary. I'd try to make fifty ticks, then one hundred ticks, then five hundred ticks. But now, when I think of my goals, they're not attached to a dollar sign. It has more to do with me personally than a specific amount. So to answer your question specifically, I start each day with a goal to be positive, confident, and consistent.

I try to make my first trade a winner. If that means I

have to wait forty-five minutes, that's the discipline. I think for me that it's important to feel good after that first trade. It gives me confidence and, I believe, sets the tone for the rest of the session.

Q: Tom, do you think having a high level of confidence when you trade is important?

Tom: It's essential. I think my confidence level is always up. I firmly believe that you have to constantly have a very positive attitude about your trading. I find, for whatever reason, if my attitude is not there, chances are I'm going to lose money for the day. So I try to pump myself up and keep my confidence level high. And if I can't, I either take a break or go home.

Q: How do you get your confidence level up?

Tom: I self-motivate. I keep talking to myself.

People outside this business don't realize the hard work and the commitment that goes into becoming a successful trader. A lot of people just think that traders show up and make numbers with a lot of zeros at the end of them by standing in the trading pit. I mean they don't realize the sacrifices and discipline that go into becoming a good trader.

You've got to constantly get yourself up psychologically. I can't see how you can do well at trading without that aspect. It literally took me years as a trader to recognize the importance of the mental side of this game. You are always competing with incredible talent. This is the big league. You must be prepared physically and mentally. So I'm constantly motivating myself, believing that I am the best one out of the hundreds of traders in the pit. I remind myself of my prior successes and my future achievements. To be successful, I think you really need to be able to taste success!

Q: When you are motivating yourself, do you see something from your childhood or some athletic figure? Do you hear something specific in your mind, some particularly inspiring words? What are you imagining in your own mind?

Tom: My daughter is the inspiration of my life. I think when I need to get myself up, I just start focusing on her. I can see her face and hear her voice. That usually gets me back to a level where I can compete.

Q: So when you see a picture of your daughter in your own mind, and hear her voice, that gets you up and you feel good?

Tom: Absolutely. If I made a series of bad trades and I'm kind of getting myself into a depressed state of mind, I will think of the last words she said to me today before I left. For me, it's just the simple things in life that motivate me. Sounds corny, huh?

Q: Tom, I think many traders underestimate that effect, not only on trading but on general performance and well-being. We create the internal environment to achieve.

Tom: Exactly. To me, motivation means something to inspire you. It makes no difference if it's a Baby Ruth bar or a child, as in my case. If you can learn how to tap into that positive thought stream, you will see that things begin to click for you. You can make yourself trade better and more aggressively. I think that was my secret for being able to step up, to keep taking my trading to the next level.

Q: Tom, how did you develop your trading method?

Tom: Here comes a very big word, but for my money, this is it in a nut shell: discipline. Without discipline there is only loss and frustration. You must develop a working code or strategy, and the discipline is your compass to stay on track. To be motivated and execute—after a while, it all becomes intuitive.

Q: So the discipline is not to waver from your trading rules?

Tom: No. You have to begin with the assumption that your trading rules will structure your trading, but the discipline is never to let your temper or your frustrations get in the way of your trading. That's why I said before that my first trade is so important to me. It sets a psychological tone for the rest of my day. The discipline is developing a mental attitude where your motivation and skill level are unstoppable.

Q: And focused.

Tom: Yes, you have to keep focused. You have to stay within what you know works for you.

Q: Can you cite an example of something that occurred to you recently on the trading floor where your focus was distracted or destroyed and how you were able to maintain your discipline and stay in tune with the market? I think this will be helpful to other traders who experience myriad disturbances and interruptions, both imagined and real, all the time.

Tom: Just yesterday, I bought five hundred contracts from a broker. At first the market was going my way. Then suddenly the market stalled and reversed slightly. I was still bullish. The broker had a thousand to sell at the market. I wanted to buy some more, but he literally ignored me and sold them at a better price to someone who was standing next to him who bid after me.

Q: He went around you.

Tom: Right. Never even looked at me.

Q: And you were the first bid?

Tom: Of course. I strongly felt pit etiquette entitled me to all or most of that order. I found myself getting caught up yelling at him, taking my focus away from the market. What happened to me was instead of trading the market I found myself focusing on that trade, rather than concentrating on what was going on. The discipline was to let go and realize that always staying in tune on a practical level is much more to my benefit than letting an event dictate my mood.

Q: So how do you get your focus back in situations like that?

Tom: I just intuitively refocus and know the right thing to do. The answer is simple. Quit arguing, Tom, and start trading!

Q: How did you learn that?

Tom: Some people learn quicker than others. As I said before, it took me a lot of years to learn that. Look around the pit. There are people who will argue about something in a heartbeat. I'm not there to be distracted. I'm here for one reason only: to trade.

There just comes a time in your life where you decide or identify what you have to do to be successful in this business. Next comes the hard part. You choose to do what works, or you can continue to do what you've been doing before. I found bitching and moaning doesn't work for me!

Q: You are saying at some point you just recognized that there was no viability to arguing with the brokers about trades, even if you were first or you were the first bid.

Tom: The arguing gets you nowhere except a lot of oohs and ahhs from the other traders who are watching you.

Q: Tom, could you describe some of the mistakes that you've made throughout your career that have served as a learning experience?

Tom: I'm glad you asked that question. Mistakes are a tremendous opportunity to learn about yourself and the market. Most people try to shove their mistakes under a rug. Again, it's all about attitude. I've always tried to focus on what I was doing wrong to learn how to do what is right. If I told you what it has taken me years and years to learn, I swear you would look at me and say that's it. For example, never fight the market. Now, doesn't that sound simple. Hey, its not rocket science, but do you know how long it took me to learn about that? Actually, I shouldn't say learn it, I should say know it! You have to know intuitively. If everybody and his brother says the market's going higher, but it keeps going lower, you can't buy it. Even though you want it down to your toes to go higher, it's not going to happen. It is such a cliche, but the trend is your friend. I've witnessed bull and bear markets, and this axiom is a constant. You may be right for a day, week, or month. But if you buck the trend, you will get nailed.

As a local, you stand in the pit and the paper keeps buying, and because you are a local trying to get the edge, you find yourself selling. But when the trend is up and the funds are buying, it's a lot easier to join them and become a buyer rather than to keep trying to make a few ticks on the short side. For many years my mistake was to not be aware of, or go against, the trend of the market. If you go with the trend, life is so much easier. It sounds awfully simple, doesn't it? But how many traders can really do it? Very few.

Q: Tom, does it bother you to lose?

Tom: No. It does not bother me to lose because I accept it as part of the business.

Q: Part of the trading process?

Tom: If I lose because I let my attitude get in my way, that bothers me. If I lose because I'm on the wrong side of the market, it doesn't bother me at all. As I said, I'm dedicated to learning from my mistakes. Losing is just part of the game. If you are afraid to lose, you shouldn't trade.

Q: Tom, why do you believe you've done so well as a trader?

Tom: I think, as I said before, that it has a lot to do with attitude. I have the ability to get beyond my frustrations or other distractions in the market and focus. I also have the discipline to keep learning from my mistakes. I've learned the ropes, and I'm prepared every second that I'm on the floor to play the game, full out.

Q: Preparation really is a big part of it, isn't it?

Tom: The whole basis of open outcry is competition. Competition is something I thrive on. I like to feel, no matter how many people are on the floor, I am one of the quickest, one of the best. I don't say this in a conceited way. I mean I just have that pumped up level of confidence that I'm here and I'm a player.

Q: So if I understand you correctly, it is constantly striving to be the best?

Tom: Yes, to be the best of the bunch. Something like that. Also I just love being here. All the markets that I've been involved in—Eurodollars, bonds, currencies—are markets that are watched throughout the world. After making a trade and calling it up on the floor and it's the high or low of the day, and reading the newspaper the next day, I like to say to myself, "Oh, that eight trade, that was me! I sold those or I bought those." For me, that is a tremendous high. The mystique of knowing the whole world is watching what we're doing and just to be a part of it. To know also that I'm always giving it my very best shot.

Q: Tom, what do you feel are the essential characteristics of a successful trader?

Tom: You can't be afraid to take the loss. In fact, at times, you have to want to take the loss.

I believe another characteristic of a successful trader is: you really have to want to play to engage yourself in trading. You see it on the trading floor. Some guys have shaved their heads or will wear flowered jackets. They want the attention. They want the brokers to give them notice. They are sending out a message that they are there to trade aggressively. We have all seen this on the floor: guys bid and offer and taunt other traders to hurt them. They are there to play.

Q: So the winning traders, in your opinion, like to stand out.

Tom: Exactly. You have to be physical when the time comes to be physical. You cannot allow yourself to be walked on; you're going to find a lot of people willing to do that to you: your broker, your clearinghouse, who knows. So I think another characteristic is the ability to stand your ground, stick up for yourself and be independent minded in every sense, relying on your own judgment.

Q: Tom, have you ever gone through a prolonged period where your trading was out of step or where you had a series of bad trades?

Tom: I had a very hard time in 1992. It was at the time the interest rate markets bottomed out and, for me at least, weren't showing any desire to go up. My trading was really dry because my market was dead. I decided to trade markets with greater volatility: the currencies and the S&P 500. It lifted my morale to know I could switch pits and make money. Before I switched, for almost a whole year, I was pretty much down.

Q: What was it like going from a two- to three-tick range market like the Eurodollars into something like the yen.

Tom: It was like trading a schizophrenic mind. But that's where the discipline comes in. I went from trading my usual number in the Euros (five hundred to a thousand) to just being another trader. The discipline was not to let ego intrude on my trading.

Q: You had to cut down your size?

Tom: Yes, I started trading one lots sometimes. I never accumulated a position of more than twenty currencies or S&Ps.

Q: Did you do well in those other markets?

Tom: Yes. The most important thing, as I alluded to before, was it kept my morale high. It allowed me to come in every day and know I could make money. In essence, the experience helped me preserve my confidence.

    I have learned a tremendous amount from that experience. Coming off a down year, I learned I had the resilience, strength, and confidence to come back. I really learned the importance of mental preparation. That is the formula I use today whenever I take a few hits in a row or I have a series of losing days. I just figure out a way to get back on track. I just know how important my confidence level is, and it is a reflection of being calm and relaxed. I just try to take each day as it comes.

Q: And how do you start each day?

Tom: As I said already, I always start every day with a positive attitude. Every day is a new day. I try not to look back on or concentrate on negative things. If you do that, you're going to have a negative attitude. So if I'm in a trading slump, I try not to focus on the slump. I concentrate only on what's positive in my attitude and my trading method. What happens invariably is, all of a sudden I make the good trade and my confidence level rebuilds itself.

Q: You know, Tom, there's a whole body of research that relates peak performance in sports to one's personal psychology: attitude, motivation, goals, beliefs, and anxiety control. Do you believe that same relationship holds true for trading?

Tom: I believe unquestionably that there is a link between the two. When I look back on my days playing football and baseball, motivation and focus are key. Since I have a history of playing competitive sports, I know you have to pay the price if you want to win. Trading is no different. I think the analogy also applies to intuition.

In the same way you develop a capacity to anticipate in sports when you play calm and relaxed, that too applies to trading. You have to learn how to get in touch with the way you're personally feeling the market. The intuition grows out of being able to monitor yourself and know how you feel about that particular market situation. You have to know the difference between a trade that feels right and one that feels wrong. I don't think any book or person can teach that. It comes from a lot of experience and desire to learn.

Q: Could you talk a little more about your view of intuition growing out of experience?

Tom: I think intuition is at the heart of trading. It takes many years to develop it so that you can use it effectively in the market. That is why I think it is such a joke when people buy a trading system or read a book on trading and say they are real intuitive about a particular trade. From my point of view, you have to earn intuition. It comes from years of day-to-day experience with the markets and an understanding of your reactions to a host of market situations.

Q: Tom, how much of your trading would you characterize as being intuitive?

Tom: You have to know the technicals of your market, but I could say just about all my trading comes down to intuition. My decisions are based on how I am feeling internally, my physical sensations as to whether the trade feels right.

Q: Tom, do you think this is true of most of the top traders?

Tom: Absolutely. I've been on the floor for many years. I've witnessed some of the greats. In the final analysis I don't think any of them rely on their charts. A great trader knows intuitively what kind of trade he is in.

Q: Are you saying the great traders are not pure technicians?

Tom: Yes. And that's not to say you can't be successful as a technician, but I believe without hesitation that the best are all intuitive traders. I think it's like the best in anything. Think about it. Where does it come from? In my experience, it's usually from imagination or creativity as a result of really knowing whatever you do well. Charts will help you, but my money is on intuition. I should be clear that I'm not telling a new trader to start thinking creatively about trading the yen. You have to put in the hours, days, weeks, months, and years of hard work. You will have to make the sacrifices. But if you plant the seed and water the plant, a flower will grow.

Chapter Eleven

Peter Mulmat

Peter Mulmat has been a member of the International Monetary Market of the Chicago Mercantile Exchange since 1982. He has actively traded on the floor of the exchange and from his office for his personal account for the last thirteen years. Mr. Mulmat's trading experience includes trading futures and options on foreign currencies, interest rate products, stock indices, grains, meats, and metals.

Mr. Mulmat has served on several important CME committees, including Foreign Exchange and Floor Practices. He currently serves as a member of the President's Council of the Museum of Science and Industry of Chicago.

Q: As the third generation of a family of traders, Peter, your background is unique.

Peter: I was born and raised in a trading environment. My grandfather, as you know, was a founding member of the Chicago Mercantile Exchange. He was in the wholesale butter and egg business back in the 1920s when the exchange was founded. It was a natural transition for him to go into the futures business. My grandfather passed away several years ago. He was 94 years old. He died, believe it or not, with a belly position still in his trading account.

Q: How many years had he traded?

Peter: He traded successfully for over sixty years. My father was also a livestock trader for many years. I learned a lot from both of them. I started working on the exchange floor when I was 15, working for my dad in the summertime, helping him hold his deck and organize his brokerage papers. Through my junior and senior years of college, I started to trade for myself in the Swiss franc pit. I was very fortunate in the sense that, when I started to trade, a busy day was six thousand contracts, and there were only two dozen traders in the pit at the time. So we'd all look at each other like we had just dealt with the world. The point I'm making is the atmosphere was conducive to learning.

Q: Any particular trading lessons you remember learning or hearing about from your grandfather or father?

Peter: There is a funny story that I would like to share with you. It has to do with my grandfather who was a well-known "ag" trader. I had been trading for two weeks. My busiest day I think I traded eight buys and eight sells. My grandfather came over to me and said, "Peter, sell the pork bellies, they're going down." I had studied international economics and finance in college so I didn't know anything about pork bellies and was absolutely terrified.

Q: So what happened?

Peter: At first, nothing. I was too nervous to make a move. After much prodding by my grandfather, I sold five contracts. I think they were August bellies at 76 and a quarter. Two days later the bellies went down to 74 cents. I immediately bought them back. I made two dollars and 25 cents a contract. I made $4000, and I was on cloud nine. Six weeks later the bellies are trading at 28 cents. My grandfather comes up to me on the exchange floor and says, "Peter, I think this is a good time to cover. Buy your bellies back in." When I told him I had left 50 cents a contract ($20,000) on the table, it was like I had carved out a piece of his heart.

Q: Peter, would you say your grandfather taught you the need to be more patient, to look to capture the trend?

Peter: Yes, of course. But in a very real sense, I think it's a comparison of apples and oranges. The tactics that work in the agriculture market often don't apply to the foreign currencies or the interest rate markets. We're not seeing rates having that kind of extreme movement. We're not seeing the dollar mark go from 320 to 150 in six weeks' time. I guess what I'm saying is, the kind of volatile moves that characterize the ag markets very often are not a good basis for understanding or trading the currencies, bonds, or S&P 500.

Q: Are you saying that the nature of the trade is different?

Peter: I think it's much different. The livestock, in my opinion, is traded by a group of people who in fact seem to do it successfully over time. I believe it is much more of a vertically rather than a horizontally integrated market. The ag traders have a more hermetic understanding of the cash and delivery and everything else. They seem to know what is going on and all the eventualities of their market. They seem to have a good grasp of the news before it happens. So I think that type of trading really doesn't apply to what I'm currently doing. There are just too many variables that are beyond the participant's grasp.

Q: Could you talk a little bit about how you developed your own trading method and what is the basis of your buying and selling decisions?

Peter: As you know, Bob, I started out as a scalper in the pits. And luckily I was able to grow as the markets grew. I can still remember the first day I made forty ticks ($500). I left the exchange walking on a cloud. You couldn't knock me down with a two-by-four I was so excited!

Q: What year was that?

Peter: Nineteen eighty. I was probably 21 years old at the time.
                When you are scalping in and out of the market, day in and day out, buying and selling with the banks and institutions, you develop a feel for the market. You start

to notice certain distinct market dynamics that tend to repeat themselves over time.

I think one of the reasons why, currently, trading seems more difficult is these dynamics are changing. Of course, they always have, but now they are doing it weekly or monthly, sometimes on a daily basis, in comparison to years at a time in the past.

You used to be able to buy on strength and sell on weakness. You also used to be able to add on strength in proportional ways that just don't work anymore.

So you have to be able to look with flexibility at a whole set of different parameters today than you used to look at in the past. You have to become aware of this shift, particularly in terms of exposure.

Q: Peter, in broad terms, what is the basis of your current trading strategy?

Peter: It's funny that you should ask that. Dave Silverman (independent currency trader and CME director) and I have been talking about this in relation to the fund we're setting up. One of the things that I think you need to do in today's environment is look at everything much more defensively. I don't mean you should trade laid back, but you definitely need to adopt a more surgical approach. I think as soon as you get in, when you're starting to build a position, you have to know where are you going to get out.

It used to be you'd come down every day and the question was, "How much are you going to make?" You looked at it very, very aggressively and very offensively. You looked at areas to exploit where the market was vulnerable. And you could push a position, really play the leverage.

I don't think that strategy works anymore. You must be aware of what's going on overnight too.

Q: What are you now trading primarily?

Peter: Japanese yen, Canadian dollars, Australian dollars,

bonds, and S&Ps. The bulk of my business is still in the
currency markets.

Q: Are you currently trading for daily or weekly moves?

Peter: You know, Bob, I'll trade an idea. I'll look for a daily
move; however, I'll certainly trade around the position,
taking advantage of the long-term trend. If I believe the
market is really undervalued or overvalued, I'll liquidate
all or part of the position and actually turn myself around
looking for a dip or short-term bounce. But, in general,
I'm always cognizant of which way I want to be in the
market.

Q: Do you use options or do you mainly restrict yourself to
futures?

Peter: I'm currently not using the options as a trading vehicle,
but at the same time I pay a lot of attention to the vola-
tilities. I watch the volatility as an indication of direction.
I'm aware of where the option traders believe the market
is under- or overvalued.

Q: What else are you looking at?

Peter: As I said before, you need the flexibility to adjust to know
what is and is not important to drive markets, and that
is always changing. Ten years ago it was gold and the
money supply. Five years ago it was the trade balance.
Now it's retail sales or durable goods. I think that you
have to weigh your opinion against what the market is
looking for at the same time. You may not believe they
are valid numbers that are determinants of what the direction or magnitude of the market should be. Nonetheless, you can't discount the fact that the market is taking
them into account. So, personally, I don't use options in
my trading strategies, but I do use them as an indication
of market direction or which way the market is leaning.

Q: Peter, what are your current trading goals?

Peter: One of the things that David and I are working on now
is to make my style more conservative and, in fact, mar-

ketable, with the idea of setting up a fund. My returns have been real good, but there is volatility to my trading.

Q: So you want to eliminate some of the volatility?

Peter: Yes, while still trying to maintain a return of 35 percent to 50 percent.

Q: Peter, could you describe some of the mistakes that you've made in your trading in the past and how that has served as a learning experience for you?

Peter: There are mistakes every day. One of the greatest aspects of trading is that there's always another opportunity to learn about yourself and the market.

Q: Are you saying you view the whole trading process as a learning experience?

Peter: Yes. It is. The market is dynamic. If you view it as an opportunity to learn, it will provide you with an unbelievably constant source of information. One of the things that I've learned, especially in the last eighteen months, is this idea of trading more defensively and being willing, even after fundamental analysis, to take a second and third look at the charts to get an idea of where I believe value is. To determine, given my comfort level, what is the optimum position size. If everything blows up in my face, I want to know where I am getting out.

My problem this year in February and March was that I was very stubborn in getting short dollars. I was long dollars and kept adding to it. I just didn't believe the currencies were at realistic levels.

I think one thing the last move has taught me is that "realistic," at best, is a relative term. I was just telling a friend of mine back in New York that I could see dollar/yen at 60. It doesn't mean it's going to be there, but it can get there! I didn't think dollar/yen would take out $90, let alone go down to $79.50. The point is, when you are wrong you can always get out and put the trade back on later or in the near term go the other way. You must not get yourself into a situation where you've committed yourself so heavily to a play where there's no acceptable place to get out.

Right now as we are speaking I've got seven different positions on. I evaluate each one of those positions in terms of what I like to call the "quality of the position." The quality is determined by my feeling of the strength of the move, the direction I believe it's going to go, and, most importantly, the location from where I have established the trade. I also look at where the market is currently and how this position relates to the other trades I have on. From this perspective, the quality of the position will determine how aggressive I am in maintaining the position, if I'm initially wrong. It will determine if I'm going to add to the position once or twice. Also, if I'm wrong where I am going, will I get out and possibly turn myself around?

Q: Peter, will you add to a losing position?

Peter: Yes, recently what I have been doing is adding once and then using a very close stop.

Q: As you know, Peter, most traders will say categorically that they never add to a loss. Have you figured out a way to go against that axiom and add profitably?

Peter: Yes. I think I have. However, I add much more aggressively when I'm right! But I will add once, sometimes twice. A lot depends on the volatility of the market I'm trading. Also part of my strategy is not to put everything on at one time. So when I say I'm adding to a loser, say I want to be long fifty or one hundred D mark and I have a good feeling about what I believe to be the direction, I will grow into the position. I'm also watching the tone and activity in the market.

Q: Will you buy a descending market or will you wait until the market has established a bottom?

Peter: I'll buy the market as it's falling, then buy more if I think a low has been made. I'll be very careful not to put my entire position on at one level. I like to have the trade a little spread out in terms of location.

I think the worst thing you can do is put everything on at one price. This is what I think you're talking about in terms of the axiom of not adding to a loser. I'm not just buying to pick a bottom. I'm selecting an area to initiate a trade in the market based on what I perceive to be value, given the current volatility.

Q: And just adding to pick a bottom . . .

Peter: There's no percentage in it. There's no good place to get out. So I think in essence what I like to do is buy a third of my position at a time, and I'll use a stop based on time of entry.

Q: Peter, if you're trading D marks and you buy the first unit of your position and the market doesn't hold your points, will you wait till the market goes to another support level before you try entering on the long side again?

Peter: It depends on a number of things: on what the other currencies are doing, on how strongly I feel about the quality of the position.

Time is also very important. It depends on how long it stays there. If the market takes another dip down and all the other currencies are holding, I'm usually pretty comfortable with the position; and if it's against strong support within a band or area of support on the chart, I'll probably add some more. But I expect within a period of time, say ten or fifteen minutes, to see that market back up to my original entry level. If the position just sits there for a longer period of time, I consider the position starting to get stale. I will start to think about where to liquidate. Of course, most of these decisions are purely intuitive. After a while you just know how long a trade should sit there before it makes its move.

Q: What percentage of your trading is day trading?

Peter: It's really difficult to say because, the way I'm trading, I'm always either long or short. I'm always involved in the market. Even when I am looking for a long-term trend, I'm trying to capitalize on intraday market movements. I'll turn my position around just because I think the markets can bounce a little bit.

Q: Peter, you have made the transition from being one of the largest locals in the currencies to becoming a successful off-floor trader. What has the change been like?

Peter: Depends on what day you ask me.

Q: Today. Has your floor experience helped or hindered your current activity?

Peter: It's interesting. There is more you get from the floor than just the physical presence of being there. Many times I believe trading in front of a screen is more difficult if your background and experience are exclusively floor trading. Initially I found one of the hardest things to do was to cut my losses and get out. One of the reasons it sounds awfully simplistic is that when you're on the floor and you're wrong and the market is moving against you, there is a tremendous amount of noise. There's drive, there's emotion that forces you out of the trade. When you're up in the office, all you see is a little line on the chart, a flash on your screen. It doesn't seem to give, at least not for me, the emotion and, consequently, doesn't generate the discomfort that motivates me to exit the position.

Q: Does it bother you when you lose?

Peter: It depends. I know the one thing you don't want to do is get emotional. The problem arises when you get yourself into a situation where you're pushing the leverage with poor location and there is no good place to get out. If you get flustered and emotional, you are going to make bad choices.

If I stick to my original strategy and the trades don't work out, I can live with that. It's the times when I relax my discipline and become emotional that I make bad decisions. So I make an effort to keep my emotions out of it as much as I can.

Q: How do you do that, Peter?

Peter: That's a very good question. I've learned how to do this as a result of going through several good and bad streaks. I believe you have to go through a consistent process of self-evaluation in order to keep yourself in check. The times when your thinking is right, your trading is just phenomenal. And then, and it happens to all of us, if you let your psychological guard down, the whole thing blows up in your face. You know what I'm talking about. That's why it is so important to constantly do this self-analysis and review what you're thinking about. And never to lose sight of the fact that the scenario you have built in your mind around your positions can change dramatically at any time. If you can maintain your poise emotionally under market conditions, there are tremendous opportunities to be gained.

Q: Peter, you've known many successful traders, some of whom are your relatives and friends. What do you think are the characteristics of successful trading?

Peter: The obvious one, of course, is intelligence and, I guess on the floor, youth and agility. But also, I think there's a drive. The best traders need to be challenged. They bring a certain exhilaration, if you will, to the risk and the rewards that are involved. They also want immediate and honest feedback. They are prepared for reward or punishment and know how to deal with both. I also find that the people who really do well at trading are goal oriented, thrive on the challenge, and are willing to work hard. They excel under pressure and, in fact, seem to enjoy it.

Many people have an incorrect perception of trading. They think you just start trading and fill your wheelbarrow up with money.

One of the lessons that I learned when I started out on the floor was you needed to be there and you needed to be there all the time. When I was a novice trader, I found that I did my best in the afternoon when some of the larger traders would leave. I could move up a little closer to the order fillers. And that was some of the best learning time I had down on the floor.

Q: In my day, Peter, I didn't know any new trader who didn't go bell to bell. I mean, that was what you did or you didn't survive!

Peter: Bob, I remember starting out when I was 15 years old; I just immediately fell in love with this place. It was very exciting, and the potential screams out at you. You're limited only by your own abilities. When I started, for the first five years all I did was study technical analysis. I took every class that was available on the markets. In college, I majored in international economics with an eye on learning how to trade. It was wonderful to see academic learning that could be readily applied. The point is, you've got to love it and work hard.

This really should come as no surprise to anyone. To be successful over a period of time, you have to be armed with the proper educational tools. You have to understand the concepts behind what you're trading and the concepts behind what everyone else that you're competing against—the MBA at Chase, at Chemical, and Bankers—is looking at. They all are armed with the best information available. They're briefed by the best staff possible. If you don't get yourself in that league, you may have some brief periods of winning trades, but the ability to maintain a consistent stream of top performance will be impossible.

Q: Have you ever figured out what percentage of your trades are profitable?

Peter: No, I haven't. I just look in terms of monthly performance. That's kind of the criteria I use to gauge my performance. I find to go any shorter period of time is just frustrating for me. And to go any longer doesn't seem to serve a purpose. I think a rigorous monthly analysis of what I've done, looking at each market individually, tends to give me a good idea of where I need to make adjustments.

Q: Do you think successful traders have a particular mind-set?

Peter: Yes. Absolutely! To be successful, you have to constantly be willing to reevaluate what you're doing and be innovative in your trading ideas. I think the most successful traders are always retooling their market theories. They are always readjusting their strategies to current conditions and perceptions. I think everyone else is kind of one step behind. You need to be able to first identify what's absolutely relevant right now. It may be different tomorrow. The worst thing you can do is become complacent. You have to be able to challenge yourself, as I said before. There are always ways to improve on what you're doing and the methodology by which you do it.

This does not only mean looking at new markets to trade and looking at new ways to trade. For currency traders it may mean just trading during the day or taking advantage of options to hedge positions.

I think you have to be willing to innovate and to constantly be committed to look ahead. Of course, the worst thing to do is to grasp on to what people are doing right now and feel that this will make you successful. You must learn to identify and trust your trading intuition.

Q: Peter, where in your opinion does your market intuition come from?

Peter: I believe intuition comes with and from experience. Markets change. The dynamics change. Patterns change, but the human reactions of people, the emotions, the movement of the markets are the same within certain parameters over time. I think experience teaches you this. You learn to think and act intuitively.

You learn intuitively what other traders, the Fed, the large institutions are focusing on. Intuition gives you the ability to act effectively, but it takes time and experience.

I haven't seen anyone come down the first day and just look at the market and rack up.

Q: So you are saying all the hard work and experience give you intuition?

Peter: Yes. There are things that I did when I started out that today I now call intuition. For example, when I first started trading in the pit, I would use a point and figure chart. A one-by-three or a two-by-six chart. What that did for me was help visualize the highs and lows for the day or when the trend lines were being touched. Today I sense the same things or feel them. There is the intuition.

You see, Bob, after using this method for a long time, I'd get to a point where the natural market flow was just stored in my brain. I learned to act on the strength of that flow and base many of my decisions, really intuitions, on the quality of that flow. I would see who was buying and who was selling and at what levels they were doing it.

Q: Which is to say that you became intuitive about the characteristics of a normal day, so when you're in an extraordinary situation, you just naturally adjust to it?

Peter: I think really what your intuition allows you to do, to put it simply, is just get in sync with the market.

Q: I guess one of the key points from your perspective is that there's really no shortcut to becoming an intuitive trader. If you haven't the experience or haven't put in the time, don't consider betting heavily on your premonitions about the S&P market.

Peter: I think the best definition for intuition that I could give is that it is a reflection of everything you've learned to do over time. Your intuition accesses information quicker and less consciously than you were able to do when you started. You don't have to look at your point and figure chart or the small insignificant market moves. You're monitoring yourself and the market. It is a process of unconsciously synthesizing a lot of different information. I also believe the more you do it, the better your intuition becomes.

Q: It develops because you give credence to it as an important source of information?

Peter: Right. And I think you're able to process all that information in a way that becomes second nature. Over time you keep increasing your ability at retrieving it, being able to act on that information effectively.

I think your intuition continues to grow from having confidence and trust in those feelings when they appear. I also think if you stop trusting yourself, you lose confidence. Then the intuition becomes stale or stops unless you're able to evolve, to keep the process dynamic because you're not adapting to the ever-changing dynamics of the marketplace.

Q: Peter, what would be your recommendation to a new trader?

Peter: First of all, not to get discouraged. There is still a tremendous amount of opportunity. I know a lot of people over the last few years have had a lot of difficulty. I'd say when I started fourteen years ago, out of every ten traders who started, maybe two would leave after six months because they just didn't do well. And maybe after a year, another three left. I'd say today, out of ten traders that start, after six months maybe two are left. It's much more difficult now than it was even five years ago. And that is exactly why it is so crucial to prepare yourself.

Q: And be prepared to work hard?

Peter: Be prepared to work very hard. Be prepared to arm yourself with the educational quantitative tools you need to be able to succeed at trading. Remember the people you're competing against. And it is a competition. You're going against the very best! Like any other competition, be it athletic or scholastic, you won't place in the top unless you're willing to prepare yourself.

Q: And the intuition will grow from all the preparation?

Peter: I believe that very much to be true. And once you develop
                mastery of specific trading skills, go back and do a very
                critical self-evaluation. Determine what tools are work-
                ing. What are the new tools that you will need to learn?
                Ask yourself what you can do to evolve your trading
                strategies. It's an ongoing process. But the key point is
                always the same: the intuition comes with preparation
                and hard work. It is the dividend you receive from your
                investment in yourself!

PART IV
USING INTUITION TO ENHANCE YOUR
TRADING PERFORMANCE

Chapter Twelve

Creating an Expectation for Trading Success

Nature's way is simple and easy but men prefer the intricate and artificial.

—Lao Tzu

The peak performance expert Dennis Waitley writes, "If it's going to be, it's up to me." All triumphs and tragedies in the market and elsewhere begin with taking responsibility for your own actions. My grandfather used to say, "The psychologically rich keep getting richer and the psychologically poor get poorer." Traders who are open minded and flexible in their approach can't help but improve. It's the result of their natural commitment to themselves and their passion for trading. When Jack Schwager interviewed Ed Seykota (*Market Wizards*, Harper Business, 1989) he asked him what a losing trader can do to transform himself into a winning trader. Seykota's response was right on the mark when he answered, "A losing trader can do little to transform himself into a winning trader. A losing trader is not going to want to transform himself. That's the kind of thing winning traders do."

Ed Toppel has stated (*Zen and the Markets*, Warner, 1992) that successful trading boils down to the following simple rules.

1. Never add to a loser.
2. Only add to a winner.
3. Let profits run.
4. Cut losses fast.

5. Don't pick tops.
6. Don't pick bottoms.
7. Let the market, not your ego, make the decisions.

It is obvious by now that what makes trading so difficult is learning how to apply these rules consistently and profitably. Toppel also writes, "There is something within each of us that has a power over our minds that prevents our acting according to what we have agreed is the proper course of action. That something is present in all of us and is very powerful, more powerful than anything I know. . . . Those who rid themselves of their egos are rewarded greatly. They are the superstars of their fields. In the markets rewards come in the form of profits. In the world of art masterpieces are the results. In sports the players are all-stars and command enormous salaries. Every pursuit has its own manifestation of victory over the ego."

Intuition in trading is the result of years of hard work, discipline, and practice—intensity fueled by commitment and desire to achieve excellence. We are blessed with limitless minds that provide us limitless opportunities to cultivate our full potential. In *The Engine of Reason, The Seat of the Soul, A Philosophical Journey into the Brain* (Bradford, 1995), Paul M. Churchland states, "The human brain, with a volume of roughly a quart, encompasses a space of conceptual and cognitive possibilities that is larger, by one measure at least, than the entire astronomical universe. It has this striking feature because it exploits the combinatories of its 100 billion neurons and their 100 trillion synaptic connections with each other. Each cell to cell connection can be strong, or weak, or anything in between . . . . If we assume, conservatively, that each synaptic connection might have any of ten different strengths, then the total number of distinct possible configurations of synaptic weights that the brain might assume is, very roughly, 10 raised to the 100 trillionth power. Compare this with the measure of only 10 to the 87th cubic meters standardly estimated for the volume of the entire astronomical universe."

As we think about reaching our full potential, it is important for us to remember this and the many things that are truly within our control. We can control our thinking if we take the time to become aware of the thoughts we are processing and assume responsibility for them. We can control our beliefs and the way we imagine ourselves. We can control the way we conceptualize the world and visualize our future in it. We can control the goals we set for ourselves and the steps we take to achieve them. We can control the way we allocate our time and the way we spend our day. We can control what is important to us, who we associate with, and what is the focus of our attention. We can control the environment we learn and live in. We can control our response to situations and circumstances, in and out of the markets, that influence our thinking and behavior. We can control the intensity, fun, and desire we bring to all our efforts. To a very real extent we are the captains of our ships and the masters of our own souls.

When you change your thinking, you change your beliefs; when you change your beliefs, you change your expectations; when you change your expectations, you change your attitude; when you change your attitude, you change your behavior; when you change your behavior, you change your performance; when you change your performance, you change your LIFE!
—*Dr. Walter D. Staples* (Wilshire, 1991)

Intuitive trading is the end product (there really is no end) of all the self-effort, desire, and commitment to improve. Intuition, that is, creativity of thought, projects itself naturally and effortlessly, optimistically, from a state of mind that is relaxed, confident, and available!

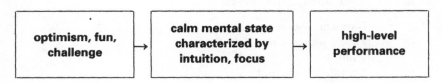

Low-level performance results from states of mind that are anxious, negative, and unavailable.

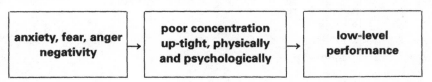

The important point here is that creativity of thought and action is the direct result, quite simply, of feeling internally relaxed. In *The Inner Athlete, Reaching Your Fullest Potential* (Stillpoint, 1994), the former Olympian Dan Millman describes his discovery of the importance of intuition and a relaxed state of mind to his own athletic performance. "Beginning with standard psychological theory, I read current studies of motivation, visualization, hypnosis, conditioning, and attitude training. My understanding grew, but only in bits and pieces . . . . Eventually, I turned to my own intuition and experience for the answers I was looking for. I understood that infants learn at a remarkable pace compared to adults. I watched my little daughter, Holly, at play to see if I could discover what qualities she possessed that most adults lacked. One Sunday morning as I watched her play with the cat in the kitchen floor, my eyes darted from my daughter to the cat and back again, and a vision began to crystalize; an intuitive concept was forming in my mind about the development of talent, not just physical talent, but emotional and mental talent as well. I had noticed that Holly's approach to play was as relaxed and mindless as the cat's, and I realized that the essence of talent is not so much the presence of certain qualities but rather the absence of mental, physical, and emotional obstructions experienced by most adults."

In his ground breaking work *Flow* (Harper Collins, 1991), Mihaly Csikszentmihalyi, a psychology professor at the University of Chi-

---

Figure 12-1   Characteristics of Flow

Physical relaxation
Psychological calm
Optimism
Energized demeanor
Active engagement
Loving fun
Managed Anxiety
Effortlessness
Automatic response
Alertness
Confidence
In control
Focus

cago, interviewed thousands of people to discover the characteristics and qualities of the ideal performance state. He termed this state "flow" (see Figure 12-1). It is a unified experience of heightened focus and "flowering" (his term) in the moment where we feel total confidence and control.

According to the author, flow is characterized by mental calmness, low anxiety, automatic and effortless action, and increased alertness and attention.

As you think about this ideal performance state, see how it relates to your own trading. Ask yourself the following questions:

1. When you trade, do you feel relaxed and loose?
2. Do you feel a sense of inner quiet and calmness?
3. Do you trade anxiety-free?
4. Do you feel a high level of energy (intensity)?
5. Are you trading in the moment?
6. Are you optimistic?
7. Are you having fun (it's possible)?
8. Is your performance effortless?
9. Is your trading automatic?
10. Are you totally focused?
11. Do you trade with a strong feeling of confidence?
12. Are you in control . . . of yourself?

Consider this exchange from an interview that I conducted with Donald Sliter, the largest independent floor trader of the S&P 500 (*The Outer Game of Trading*, Irwin 1994).

Q: So for you, Don, trading is really like playing basketball. I would like to convey to our readers that, even as we're just talking about your trading, you are incredibly animated. You are almost jumping out of your seat. You're having such a good time, just talking about it. I get the feeling that trading is just a huge high for you.

Don: I'll tell you what; I get in a zone. I'll trade thousands of S&P contracts in a day, and I'm just moving in and moving out, feeling great, eating up everything in sight. . . . I get in the car in the morning and I'm juiced. I can't wait, especially on number days or on expirations. I get so pumped up sometimes . . . . Just the idea that each day is going to be different, that I'm in control of my own situation, my own destiny, every single day. There's nobody to answer to. Everything you do you're either rewarded or you're spanked for.

James E. Loehr, the eminent sports psychologist, offers a four-step program for achieving athletic excellence (*Mental Toughness Training for Sports*, Plume, 1982). It applies equally well, I believe, to trading.

Step 1. Self-discipline. This is the stage of commitment. Everything worthwhile begins at this level. Here's where you pay the price: whatever you have to do and whatever sacrifices are necessary to get the job done and reach what you see as your ultimate potential. Yes, it's hard work—it means giving up things you enjoy in order to achieve a higher goal.

Step 2. Self-control. Loehr describes this stage in the following way: "As you discipline yourself, you experience steady increases in self-control of what you do, what you think, and how you react."

Step 3. Self-confidence. Self-confidence flows naturally from a commitment to self-control. Self-confidence is an unshakable belief in yourself and your abilities, your proven market techniques, and your ability to execute flawlessly. It comes from knowing, that is, believing, that you are in control and are taking full responsibility for whatever happens.

Step 4. Self-realization. Self-realization is simply living up to your full potential as a human being and as a trader. It is accepting yourself confidently and allowing yourself to think intuitively about the market and everything else. It is in essence opening yourself consistently to all that you are capable of achieving. The famed basketball coach John Wooden described this stage well when he said, "Success is peace of mind, which is a direct result of self-satisfaction in knowing you did your best to become the best that you are capable of becoming."

It is equally important, I believe, for you as a trader to learn how to condition yourself to monitor your thoughts and actions in the market. To listen to what you're saying to yourself and thinking. To develop a tolerance and friendliness, eventually a fascination with your own inner voice. To be mindful of pessimism or negativity and replace the negative talk with something optimistic and constructive. When working with traders, I always say do not just try to break bad thoughts or habits—replace them. Figure 12-2 gives some examples of energizing thoughts.

Figure 12-2   Energizing Thoughts

1. I always give it my best shot.
2. I'm willing to pay any price to achieve my goals.
3. I play to win, I don't play "not to lose."
4. I'm going to _____ and have fun while I'm learning.
5. I'm in control . . . of myself.
6. I will be successful.

One additional point must be made here about the most effective attitude to adopt when making mistakes. If you say to yourself "Mistakes cannot be tolerated" or "I will never make mistakes" or as I've heard traders say over the years, "I'm going to punish myself for making that trade" (usually, in my experience, they end up punishing the people closest to them at that very moment), you are sure to experience frustration, disappointment, and anger. It is simply not true that to be a winner you must be perfect. A healthier and more effective attitude is the realization that in order to learn, you must make mistakes. Say to yourself,"If I don't make mistakes, I simply won't learn." Develop the confidence in yourself to know that mistakes will be at a minimum when you have created a relaxed internal state.

In *The Mental Game* (Plume, 1990), James Loehr makes this point as it relates to tennis, and I believe it applies equally well to trading: "If losing is equated with failure, the battle of confidence cannot be won. Your motto should always be, 'Win or lose, another step forward.' You can find success in a losing effort when you establish clear performance goals prior to the match. You have the potential to learn much more from a loss than a victory. When you set your goals properly, your confidence can continue to grow, independent of your match's outcome."

Figure 12-3   Characteristics of Creative Thought and Performance

- There is an optimum internal state for each trader.
- Only when the trader feels good (calm, relaxed, etc.) will performance approach optimum levels.

- Consistently high levels of successful trading performance are a direct result of the way one feels physically and psychologically at any moment in time.
- What the trader is processing internally is within his or her control.
- Competitive and sustained trading success is the ability to create internal states of mind regardless of market action.

So to review, the essential factors leading to an intuitive state of mind for the trader are the following.

- Mental relaxation
- Physical calm
- Confidence
- Optimisim
- Focus on the moment
- Energized demeanor
- High awareness and ability to let go

Mental Relaxation

In describing peak performance feelings, Dr. Charles Garfield (*Peak Performance, Mental Training Techniques of the World's Greatest Athletes,* Warner, 1984) observes "of all the feeling states examined, a sense of inner calm is by far the most frequently mentioned. Along with this inner calm, athletes often report feeling a sense of time being slowed down and having a high degree of concentration. By contrast, a loss of concentration, a sense of everything happening too fast, and a sense of things being out of control are associated with mental tension."

Payton Jordon, arguably this country's most successful Olympic track and field coach, described Olympic gold medal winning discus thrower Al Oerter as "the most mentally poised athlete" he had ever met. According to Jordon, as reported to Charles Garfield (*Peak Performance*), Oerter possessed the ability to maintain himself under the most intense competitive pressure in a state of optimal psychological readiness. I believe the description that follows offers performance insight to every trader, whether operating on the floor or in front of a screen. "I had been familiar with Oerter's athletic capabilities for a number of years. In 1967, we were both employed at the Grumman Aerospace Corporation and had worked out in our off-hours at a gym across the street from Grumman. Even watching

Oerter work out, I was always aware of his sense of reserve and self-mastery. He knew himself well, both mentally and physically, and he had an acceptance of his own limitations, though he was always pushing beyond them. He had a great ability to calmly self-criticize and self-correct. Oerter seemed to recognize fully his emotions as a source of power and inspiration that contributed to his abilities, and he knew how to direct his emotions for maximum benefit."

Maintaining the ideal performance state was not, at least for Oerter, a complicated process. He described his own athletic poise as "the ability to step outside yourself" and to calmly ask how you can correct or improve your performance. He did not struggle with his own ego to do this; such a struggle can lead to choking or to caving in under pressure. Oerter reflected that there was clearly a state of mind that made it possible for him to perform at the highest levels of which he was capable, but he expressed this in a very casual way: "As long as I can concentrate and remain calm, I can normally do very well."

What then can traders do specifically to affect their state of mind?

I would like to start off by graphically presenting what the winning state of mind looks like for the optimum performing trader (see Figures 12-4 through 12-11).

Figure 12-4   The Winning State of Mind

Resourceful State of Mind

- Calm

- Anxiety-free

- Confident ($\rightarrow$ Strategy $\rightarrow$ Positive trading response)

- High self-esteem

- Intuitive

Psychological Characteristics of the Winning State of Mind

- Expecting the best of yourself

- Optimism

- Creating an internal atmosphere for success based on compelling motivation and focus

- Communicating effectively with yourself; seeing yourself as positive, resourceful, self-empowering

Figure 12-5   Internal Processes for Enhancing State

Visual	Auditory	Kinesthetic
Brightness	Loudness	Even
Color	Duration	Warm
Contrast	Pitch	Cold
Distance	Tone	Pulsating
Location	Location	Intermittent
Shapes	Direction	Strong
Size	Rhythm	Relaxed

Figure 12-6   Visual Imagery That Enhances Trading Performance

- Picturing success
- Seeing yourself in control
- Looking competent, relaxed, positive
- Viewing a positive past visual image of yourself
- Viewing a future visual image of improved performance

Figure 12-7   Auditory Imagery That Enhances Trading Performance

- Hearing the voice of success
- Saying to yourself, "I know I was right"
- Listening to the voice of positive expectation

Figure 12-8   Kinesthetic Imagery That Enhances Trading Performance

- Body feels light, confident
- Body is energized, strong
- Focus is direct and alert
- Breathing is relaxed, effortless, long and deep

Figure 12-9   Positive Beliefs That Enhance Trading Performance

- I believe I am or will be a successful trader.
- I believe I can achieve excellent results in my trading.
- I believe I can identify and execute winning trades.
- I believe I can trade with confidence.
- I believe I can trade effortlessly and automatically.
- I believe each day's performance is fresh.
- I believe I am personally responsible for all my trades.
- I believe I can be successful without being perfect.
- I believe I learn from my mistakes.

- I believe one bad trade is just that.
- I believe trading is a process.
- I believe that by believing in myself and in my proven methodology and by approaching trading each day with a fresh, positive state of mind, I possess the ultimate trading edge.

Graphically, the syntax of optimum trading performance looks like Figure 12-10 on an objective level and Figure 12-11 on a subjective level.

Figure 12-10   The Syntax of Optimum Trading Performance—Objective

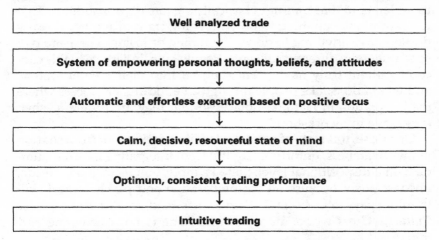

Well analyzed trade
↓
System of empowering personal thoughts, beliefs, and attitudes
↓
Automatic and effortless execution based on positive focus
↓
Calm, decisive, resourceful state of mind
↓
Optimum, consistent trading performance
↓
Intuitive trading

Figure 12-11   The Syntax of Optimum Trading Performance—Subjective

Bodily Response	Visualization	Auditory	Thoughts, attitudes, beliefs
Body feels light; shoulders are erect; torso is straight; facial muscles are relaxed; breathing is deep and full; eyes looking straight ahead—trading is feeling strong and enthusiastic.	Seeing yourself in control; relaxed, looking competent and positive; and picturing success.	Hearing the voice of confidence and control; listening to the voice of positive expectation.	Confidence, self-esteem, and self-trust—trading is anxiety free, effortless, and automatic.

Remember, we are assuming a heightened psychological state in order to execute a time-proven effective trading strategy. For the trader, this relaxed mental state of optimum trading performance allows flawless execution of a winning methodological approach that has shown consistency and reliability over time. Keep in mind the recipe for successful trading. The trader identifies an opportunity, reacts automatically, and then feels good because it was the right trade to make, true to methodology and the laws of probability.

Mark Douglas (*The Disciplined Trader*, NYIF, 1990) reaffirmed this point when I interviewed him. He stated, "Success involves learning to understand that trading is basically a game of probabilities. That it doesn't have anything to do with being right or wrong. It really doesn't have anything to do with winning or losing. These are two fundamentally different concepts. People give lip service to this concept, without truly having integrated it into their mental system, and what I do is take people through an educational process where the integration in fact takes place, so that they are different when they leave my workshop."

Of course, this state of mental relaxation derives not from sharing in this awareness, unfortunately, but from integrating internal calmness on a dispositional level. Stated simply, you feel "good" inside, unconsciously, because all the preparation and psychological skill training pays off. As D. T. Suzuki has said in *Zen and Japanese Culture*, "Great works are done when one is not calculating and thinking."

When a tennis player is on his game he's not thinking about how, when, or even where to hit the ball. He's not trying to hit the ball, and after the shot he doesn't think about how badly or how well he made contact. The ball seems to be hit through an automatic process that doesn't require thought. There may be an awareness of the sight, sound, and feel of the ball, and even of the tactical situation, but the player just seems to "know" without thinking what to do.

—Timothy Gallwey, *The Inner Game of Tennis*
(Random House, 1974)

Physical Calm

The sense of psychological relaxation moves to a physical level. Muscles are loose. Torso is erect, breathing is deep and full. All physical systems are go ahead and up and at 'em. The important points to remember here are the following.

- Tension and relaxation are mutually exclusive. It is not possible to be physically relaxed and tense simultaneously.
- It is possible to monitor your tension level on an ongoing basis to determine how tense you are feeling at any given time. Most traders do not discriminate between small increases or decreases in muscular tension. They can be taught this skill.
- Physical relaxation of the body through decreased muscular tension will enhance the trader's psychological state and reduce anxiety.
- Physical relaxation is accomplished by systematically relaxing and contracting all major muscle groups in the body.

What follows is the most utilized relaxation technique in sports. It was developed by Dr. Edmund Jacobson. It is called progressive relaxation because you progress from one muscle group to the next until the major muscle groups are converged. Jacobson's progressive relaxation involves the tensing and relaxing of specific muscles so that you develop an awareness of the difference between tension and relaxation.

The goal of this exercise is to acquire the ability to completely relax within a short period of time and eventually to be able to relax on cue in the midst of a stressful situation. I am quoting Dr. Jacobson's technique as presented in *The Mental Advantage* by Robert S. Weinberg (Leisure Press, 1988).

As you become more skilled and aware, you can omit the tension phase and just focus on relaxation.

1. Get as comfortable as possible.
   - Tight clothing should be loosened and your legs should not be crossed.
   - Take a deep breath, let it out slowly, and become as relaxed as possible.

2. Raise your arms and extend them out in front of you.
   - Now make a fist with both hands as tightly as you can.
   - Notice the uncomfortable tension in your hands and fingers.
   - Hold the tension for five seconds; then let the tension out halfway and hold for an additional five seconds.

- Notice the decrease in tension but also concentrate on the tension that is still present.
- Then let your hands relax completely.
- Notice how the tension and discomfort drain from your hands and are replaced by sensations of comfort and relaxation.
- Focus on the contrast between the tension you felt and the relaxation you now feel.
- Concentrate on relaxing your hands completely for ten to fifteen seconds.

3. Tense your upper arms hard for five seconds.
   - Focus on the feeling of tension.
   - Then let the tension out halfway for an additional five seconds.
   - Again, focus on the tension that is still present.
   - Now relax your upper arms completely for ten to fifteen seconds and focus carefully on the developing relaxation.
   - Let your arms rest limply at your sides.

4. Curl your toes as hard as possible.
   - After five seconds, relax the toes halfway and hold the reduced tension for an additional five seconds.
   - Then relax your toes completely and focus on the relaxation spreading into the toes.
   - Continue relaxing your toes for ten to fifteen seconds.

5. Point your toes away from you and tense your feet and calves.
   - Hold the tension hard for five seconds, let it out halfway for an additional five seconds.
   - Relax your feet and calves completely for ten to fifteen seconds.

6. Extend your legs and raise them approximately six inches above the floor and tense your thigh muscles.
   - Hold the tension for five seconds, let it out halfway for an additional five seconds, and then relax your thighs completely.
   - Concentrate on totally relaxing your feet, calves, and thighs for about thirty seconds.

7. Tense your buttocks for five seconds, then let the tension out halfway for another five seconds.
   - Finally, relax your buttocks completely and focus on the sensations of heaviness and relaxation.

- Concentrate on also relaxing the other muscle groups that you have already dealt with.

8. Tense your stomach muscles as hard as possible for five seconds and concentrate on the tension.
   - Then let the tension out halfway for an additional five seconds before relaxing your stomach muscles completely.
   - Focus on the spreading relaxation until your stomach muscles are completely relaxed.

9. Press the palms of your hands together and push so as to tense the chest and shoulder muscles.
   - Hold the tension for five seconds, then let the tension out halfway for an additional five seconds.
   - Now relax the muscles completely and concentrate on the relaxation until your muscles are completely loose and relaxed.
   - Concentrate also on the muscle groups that have been previously relaxed.

10. Push your shoulders back as far as possible so as to tense your back muscles.
    - Let the tension out halfway after five seconds, hold the reduced tension, and focus on it carefully for an additional five seconds.
    - Relax your back and shoulder muscles completely.
    - Focus on the spreading relaxation until they are completely relaxed.

11. While keeping the muscles of your torso, arms, and legs relaxed, tense your neck muscles by bringing your head forward until your chin digs into your chest.
    - Hold for five seconds, release the tension halfway for another five seconds, and then relax your neck completely.
    - Allow your head to hang comfortably while you focus on the relaxation developing in your neck muscles.

12. Clench your teeth and notice the tension in the muscles of your jaws.
    - After five seconds, let the tension out halfway for five seconds, and then relax completely.

- Let your mouth relax completely with your lips slightly parted and concentrate on totally relaxing these muscles for ten to fifteen seconds.

13. Tense your tongue by pushing it into the roof of your mouth as hard as possible.
    - Hold for five seconds; then let the tension out halfway, hold for an additional five seconds, and relax your tongue completely.
    - Focus now on completely relaxing the muscles of your neck, jaw, and tongue.

14. With your eyes closed, squint and rotate your eyeballs upward as if you were looking up.
    - Hold the tension for five seconds, then release it halfway for an additional five seconds.
    - Then relax your eyes completely.
    - Focus on the relaxation developing in your eyes and also concentrate on relaxing your other facial muscles.

15. Wrinkle your forehead and scalp as tightly as possible.
    - Hold the tension for five seconds, and then release halfway for another five seconds.
    - Relax your scalp and forehead completely.
    - Focus on the developing feeling of relaxation and contrast it with the tension that existed earlier.
    - Concentrate now for about a minute on relaxing all the muscles of your body.

16. Controlled breathing is one of the most important elements of the relaxation response: it is possible to bring forth a feeling of relaxation by correct breathing.
    - Take a series of short inhalations, about one per second, until the chest is filled.
    - Hold for about five seconds, then exhale slowly for about ten seconds while thinking to yourself the words "relax" or "calm."
    - Think about the word as you slowly let out your breath.
    - Repeat the process at least five times, each time striving to deepen the state of relaxation that you're experiencing.

The key point to remember here is that by continually maximizing your physical state, you will dramatically enhance your awareness of your internal state. Meditation and visualization are additional techniques that may be used by the trader. Once you "know" (intuitively) the relationships between how you feel on the inside on both a physical and psychological level, you will be in a position to optimize your performance (trading) on the outside. Your ultimate objective is to gain a high degree of control over your feelings to eliminate any internal hindrance at the moment of decision and execution.

Confidence

In *Peak Performance* (Warner, 1984), Charles A. Garfield writes "A feeling of self-confidence about being able to perform well is reported as a key factor that determines whether the athlete can transform a potentially threatening athletic challenge into a success while maintaining poise."

So what exactly is confidence? I believe confidence in its simplest terms (usually the most accurate) is no more than expecting the best of yourself and assuming a positive trading outcome in the market. Fear is just the opposite, the inablility to execute or make a trading decision (i.e., pull the trigger). It is a negative expectation of what is to come in the market before it happens.

Remember, your level of confidence is affected by your psychological and physical state. The associations, images, and attitudes you are processing in your mind are within your control. Once you become aware of what is affecting your confidence level negatively, change the imagery to something that will enhance your expectation of improved performance. One other thing needs to be mentioned. For most of us it will take time and self-acceptance to realize that confidence building is a learned skill born of experience. Yes, you will make mistakes and your confidence at times will seem to desert you, and these are the very times when the commitment, desire, and intensity to succeed will compel you to monitor your emotions and create a thought or image to boost your confidence level.

You learn to ski by skiing. You learn to trade by trading. The analogy is particularly useful when you recall learning to ski; you started on small hills and maybe even on special skis. You built up a foundation of ski experience that paved the way for blue and black diamond runs. The inexperienced trader can learn a lot about trading and risk management by trading anything or by small-stakes gambling. In fact, many of today's great traders got their starts in just this way. Contrary to what the educational process in this country has tried to get us to believe, you don't learn to live your life. You live your life and you learn.

                              —Charles Faulkner, *The Outer Game of Trading*
                                                        (Irwin, 1994)

Optimism

There is almost universal agreement among all the top traders that a feeling of optimism is key to implementing effective trading strategies. It is exactly this optimistic approach that allows traders to be able to execute the often repeated trading axiom, "Cut your losses short and let your profits run." What we are speaking of is a feeling of optimism in your abilities as a trader, the reliability of your trading method, and the benevolence (seriously) of the market to reward you for making good decisions.

Almost any book that has ever been written on trading, and lately they seem to be multiplying like rabbits on hormone injections, identifies fear and greed as the two forces that drive markets. My view is somewhat different. I believe there is just one force: GREED. However, it manifests itself in the forms of fear and hope.

Typically when a trader initiates a trade and it moves against him, he begins to hope that the trade will come back rather than fear the present loss. Conversely, when the same trader initiates a trade that goes in his favor, he fears the loss of built-up profits and moves out too quickly rather than hoping for greater profits. Most traders have it backwards. When the market is going against you is no time to hope. This is the time to fear and get out! However, when the market is moving your way is the time for optimism (hope is not a consoling word in this context). Of course, I'm assuming there was an internal logic for the initiation of this trade in the first place. By merely reversing our psychological approach in these two circumstances, we give ourselves a way of cutting our losses quickly and letting our profits build to their full potential. It is optimism that allows us to make the most of market conditions. Jack Sandner emphasized the importance of optimism when I interviewed him in *The Innergame of Trading*. He said, "I always say this is the first day of the rest of my life, and I come in optimistic with the glass half full, and I'm able to do it even if that day turns out to be negative. I start the next day by telling myself today is the first day of the rest of my life and I'm going to keep the same air of optimism, the same physiology, the same way of thinking that I had before when I was successful. I'm going to do the same successful thing."

Martin Seligman, the author of *Learned Optimism* (Random House, 1990), has conducted groundbreaking research. Seligman, who is a professor of clinical psychology at the University of Pennsylvania, has developed a typology of successful performance based on how one feels and thinks (optimistic versus pessimistic) as they relate to considerations of time, space, and person. Relating Seligman's work on optimism to optimal trading performance, consider Figure 12-12.

Figure 12-12   Characteristics of Optimistic and Pessimistic Thinking as Related to Trading

	Good Trades	Bad Trades
Optimistic	Permanent Pervasive Personal	Impermanent Isolated Impersonal
Pessimistic	Impermanent Isolated Impersonal	Permanent Pervasive Personal

I always say to myself I'm going to have a good day. And even if it isn't good, I always kind of look on the bright side of everything. I'm really the eternal optimist, which I think is essential. I mean, that's like the essential ingredient in being a good trader; you just have to be positive.

—Bruce Johnson, *The Innergame of Trading*
(Irwin, 1994)

Focus on the Moment

The key to disciplined trading is focus. Focus is a skill that can be learned based on your methodological approach to the market, what you believe about yourself, and the viability of your trading strategy. I've said before that what distinguishes the top traders is that they are conditioned, physically and psychologically, to take action in the market at their particular, often unique, point of focus. They do this with decision, without conflict or uncertainty. It is their (often unconscious) focus that allows them to identify a signal, take automatic action, and respond to whatever the result without any emotional hindrance.

All the research points to the fact that elevating your state of mind continually by focusing on internal and external phenomena that allow you to stay undistracted and true to your trading strategy is the answer. By now you know how to do this by processing positive beliefs and thoughts and by monitoring and directing your physiology. You cannot fight negative thoughts that compromise or distract your focus. Acknowledge their existence, replace them, and move forward!

To become a champion requires a condition of readiness that causes the individual to approach with pleasure even the most tedious practice session.

—James Loehr, *Mental Toughness Training for Sports*
(Plume, 1982)

Energized Demeanor

While you were trading, have you ever experienced any of the following?

- Feeling slow and heavy
- Easily distracted
- Low level of patience (itchy to do something else)
- Don't really care feeling
- Feeling exhausted, out of energy
- Feeling your timing was off (one step behind)
- Feeling bored or just generally lazy
- Feel you are out of sync, nothing seems to work

Well, so have I, and so has every other trader. The point is, the sooner you recognize your lowered energy level and respond to it during the trading session with a determination to energize yourself, the quicker you will be back on track. Consider employing some of the following strategies to reverse your energy level.

- Increase your breathing rate until you feel your energy increasing.
- Run in place.
- Jump up and down—you may look silly but you'll feel good!
- Get your body moving as much as possible to increase circulation and heart rate.

Think energizing thoughts. Consider some of the following:

- Thoughts of pride
- Thoughts of personal achievement
- Thoughts of individual excellence
- Thoughts of personal challenge
- Thoughts of the "ecstasy of winning"

Remember, at first, to process these thoughts slowly. You will literally begin to feel them stick in your mind. See them vividly. Hear them in your voice or in the voice of someone close to you. The more compelling the thoughts or image, the greater the energizing effect that will result. Some additional energizing thoughts are the following:

- Think of something that is really good in your life. See it, hear it, feel it.
- Think of something in your life that you are really proud of.
- Think of something in your life that really excites you. Begin to act the way you feel, breathe, walk, and so on when you are really excited about something.
- Think of a person in your life whom you love. See him or her, hear him or her, feel him or her.
- Think of a person who loves you.
- Think of something that's funny. See it, hear it, feel it. How does it make you feel?

I can't emphasize strongly enough the role of humor and its effect on optimum trading performance. Although it is obvious that preparation and practice don't provoke much in the way of laughter, humor will sustain an excellent result. In *Mental Toughness* (Plume, 1982), James Loehr writes, "A high positive performance occurs in a state of fun. The sense of joy that accompanies every great performance can even be accompanied by mirthful laughter." Loehr goes on to make what I believe is a striking point—that based on his research, a state of high positive humor (his term) and the intuitive state, when one is totally available to new information and creative thinking, are one and the same on a physiological and psychological level. Loehr states, "High positive humor is the optimum state; you look for humor so that you can sustain it and it can sustain you. One way to define humor is to look at it as the intersection of two thought systems, and this is also the formula for creativity. . . . The emotional constellation of the creative state (intuition) and the emotional constellation of the ideal performance state are identical."

Other energizing techniques include focusing on your most important goal. Performance goals will energize you faster than outcome goals. Review in your mind the following:

- What are my trading goals?
- Why is it important for me to achieve this goal?
- What specifically is preventing me from achieving my goals right now?
- What can I do right now to prepare mentally?
- What can I do right now to prepare physically?
- What must I do to pay the price for excellence?

As you review your goal and imagine it vividly, you will begin to feel your energy level rising to sufficiently improve your performance. In addition, you can verbally tell yourself some of the following things: "I can do it," "get energized," "yes, I can," or whatever additional internal saying works for you.

Act energized. Even though you may not feel energized, you can raise your energy level quicker by acting your way out of it than trying to wait until the feeling of low-level energy passes. By simply acting as if you really felt energized, you will activate your physiology.

It must be stated that sometimes, however hard we try, the high-level energy feeling we try to create just seems to abandon us. It just doesn't come. John Wooden used to say, "When everything else seems to desert you, remember you still have two friends in your corner: guts and determination."

High Awareness and the Ability to "Let Go"

In *Peak Performance, Mental Training Techniques of the World's Greatest Athletes* (Warner, 1984), Dr. Charles A. Garfield writes, "Athletes almost universally describe a state of mind in which they are acutely aware of their bodies and of the athletes around them and have an uncanny ability to anticipate correctly other athletes' moves and respond effectively to them . . . words such as joy, ecstasy, intensity and power are frequently used to describe this state. Although fear, anxiety and even rage have been traditionally associated with high performance levels, these feelings were rarely mentioned as contributing in any way to this high energy state."

In my interviews with top traders this state of heightened awareness, focus, and present moment orientation was repeated over and over again as a key element of optimum trading performance. I believe the key to enhancing your ability to increase awareness is to trust yourself and to believe (not intellectually) that thinking too much will inhibit you. As one NFL football player is reported to have said, "Thinking is what gets you caught from behind."

Optimum trading performance must be automatic, natural, and spontaneous. The way to achieve this state again is to relax your mind and body, by creating a resourceful state of mind where you are available for new information, intuitive and objective, and most important, by learning how to "let it happen" rather than force it to happen.

In my experience in working with traders, developing an attitude of "letting go" is often very difficult to achieve. I believe the reason for this is that it is often misperceived or confused with adopting a feeling of passivity or being laid back or somehow relying on whatever happens to you. Nothing could be farther from the truth.

To increase your level of awareness, ask yourself some of the following questions:

1. How do I feel when I'm really trading well?
2. What am I seeing at these times in my mind's eye?
3. What am I hearing in my mind's ear?
4. What am I thinking about?
5. What do I believe about myself at these times?
6. What is the best combination of winning feelings for me?

"Letting go" for the trader involves trusting his subconscious processes to perform at optimum levels, relinquishing conscious controls (i.e., second-guessing) that inhibit his trading. This trust grows out of commitment, discipline, and practice of mind-body skills.

The opposite of "letting go" is trading tight, where negative thoughts and images stimulate negative memories, associations, or future expectations and where the left hemisphere of the brain dominates the right.

Tight performance falls into five categories:

1. Trying too hard, constantly trying to make it happen.
2. Worrying about past errors and the concomitant fear of repeating those mistakes in the future.
3. Tentative or unsure execution. Straddling the fear of decision, "to trade or not to trade that is the question."
4. Becoming overly concerned with the profit or loss, making the trading decisions cautious, anxious, or mechanical (as opposed to effortless).
5. Obsessed with doing the "right thing," being conscious rather than unconsious of every move you make in the market. Every trade or tactic is a life-and-death struggle, stress-filled and unnatural.

I would like to present here three descriptions, from three different sources of what "letting go" looks and feels like:

The greatest efforts in sports come when the mind is as still as a glass lake.

— Timothy Gallway, *The Inner Game of Tennis*
(Random House, 1974)

From D. T. Suzuki (1959) on developing a "non-interfering attitude of mind:"

. . . . The mind then reaches the highest point of alacrity, ready to direct its attention anywhere it is needed—to the left, to the right, to all the directions as required. When your attention is engaged and arrested by sticking the sword of the enemy, you lose the first opportunity of making the next move by yourself. You tarry, you think, and while this deliberation goes on, your opponent is ready to strike you down. The thing is not to give him such a chance. You must follow the movement of the sword in the hands of the enemy, leaving your mind free to make its own counter movement without your interfering deliberation.

The following description of what it is like to experience the state of mind of "letting go" is based on statements of some of the world's greatest athletes that were compiled by Charles H. Garfield (*Peak Performance*):

"All at once it seems as though everything is working for me. There is no sense of needing to do anything. My actions unfold as they do in pleasant dreams, though my body may be putting out great efforts. I have no thoughts about what I should do or how I should do it. Everything is happening automatically, as though I have tuned myself in on a radio beam that directs my nervous system so that it works in synchronization with everything in and around me. I feel insulated from all distractions. Time disappears, and even though I know the speed of actions taking place around me, I feel I have all the time I need to respond accurately and well. I am so completely involved in the action that there is not even a question of confidence or the lack of it. There are no issues such as worries about failure or feelings of fatigue. Even feeling momentary fear appears to serve me, changing automatically into a positive force. Success is not an issue, though at the same time it seems natural and easy to achieve. I feel strangely detached from what I am doing even while I am completely in touch with everything, at one with my actions. The whole issue of mind and body separation seems to dissolve, as I feel that both are responding perfectly to my own wishes and inner promptings. I am acutely aware of colors, sounds, the presence of people around me, the feeling of being a source of power and energy in this moment in time. It is a trancelike state, but I feel totally in touch with everything around me, with everything within me, as though the usual barriers between me and the outside world have been peeled away, and I am completely at one with myself and the physical world with which I am interacting. It is a wonderful feeling, crisp, full of joy, more real than the everyday world, going very deep, an experience that rewards me many times over for all the effort I have put into my sport."

The important points for the trader to remember are these, as simple as they seem:

- Your trading performance is a direct reflection of how you feel internally, not the other way around. When you feel good, you perform at high levels.

- Trading performance at the highest levels occurs automatically without conscious deliberation where the right internal climate has been established, based, of course, on a proven method and technical skills.
- The trader must possess the skills necessary to create and maintain positive internal feelings regardless of the circumstances or situation:

Illustration → positive emotional state → leads to optimum trading performance

Getting Started

- Assess your current emotional state

Checklist of Personal Trading State

	1	2	3	4	5	
I usually trade relaxed.	0	0	0	0	0	anxious
I usually trade focused	0	0	0	0	0	distracted
I usually trade confident.	0	0	0	0	0	unsure
I usually trade with control.	0	0	0	0	0	no control
My trading is automatic.	0	0	0	0	0	indecisive
I trade effortlessly.	0	0	0	0	0	great effort
I trade feeling energized.	0	0	0	0	0	lethargic
I trade with positive beliefs.	0	0	0	0	0	negative
I trade with positive self-talk.	0	0	0	0	0	negative
I find trading fun.	0	0	0	0	0	labored

- Ask yourself the following questions:
- How would my trading performance be improved if I managed my emotional state?
- What has been the psychological cost of not trading in the right emotional state?
- How much more profitable would my trading be if I always traded in a positive, resourceful state of mind?
- How much more fun would I have if I constantly managed my state of mind?
- How would the intrinsic quality of my life be enhanced if I were in an optimum performance state of mind every day?

Yes, there is a lot to think about. And, remember, the goal is to get to the point that the answers are fully integrated so you don't have to think at all.

I believe the ideas that I have presented here, and I say this with great humility, represent the essence of what the internal climate of optimum trading performance feels like. If I have repeated an idea too often, it is because, based on my considerable work with traders of every stripe, orientation, and product, I have learned that there is a need for repetition of these concepts, however simple and obvious they seem. It is important for the trader to personally identify, practice, and master these concepts in order to achieve trading success. I sincerely do not think it is sufficient to present concepts or ideas of such practical importance just once, as if they are a single prize in a Cracker Jack box. The key to successful trading is always this: You must feel good to perform great. Feeling good is in your control by altering your internal state. It is the ability to change your emotional state, to move from left-brain dominance to right-brain self-realization, that will guarantee your optimum trading performance and will allow you to become an intuitive trader.

Chapter Thirteen

Motivation and Reality

To take the master's journey, you have to practice diligently, striving to hone your skills, to attain new levels of competence. But while doing so— and this is the inexorable fact of the journey—you also have to be willing to spend most of your time on a plateau, to keep practicing even when you seem to be getting nowhere.

—George Leonard, Mastery *(E. P. Dutton, 1991)*

Principles of Successful Trading

- Define your loss.
- Believe in yourself and in unlimited market possibilities.
- Have a well-defined money management program.
- Don't buy price.
- Don't buy tips.
- Don't trade angry or euphoric.
- Trade aggressively at your numbers and points.
- Focus on opportunities.
- Consistently apply your trading strategies and rules.
- Be highly motivated and goal oriented.
- The trend really is your friend.
- When in doubt, stay out.
- Don't overtrade.
- Know how to use orders.
- Never average a loss.
- Take small losses, big profits.
- Have no bias to either side of the market.
- Don't pyramid.

- The crowd is almost always wrong.
- Concentrate on one market.
- Preserve capital.
- Think in probabilities.
- Always trade in a highly positive and resourceful state of mind.
- Act in certainty.
- The market is never wrong.

Your Trading Game Plan

Always

- Rehearse mentally.
- Practice an open, flexible, nondefensive state of mind.
- Practice patience in all things; it will improve your trading.
- Pace yourself physically and emotionally.
- Remember, trading is not about proving something—to yourself or anyone else.
- Condition yourself regularly for trading success.

Motivation

Top traders are not top traders because they have inherited a top trading gene. Winners are not born, they are made. The most compelling force in your development as a trader, or as a human being for that matter, is the thinking you engage in and the beliefs about yourself and the environment you choose to accept as "real." If you do not believe in failure and deny its reality, you cannot be defeated. The only "real" limitations on what you can accomplish are those you impose on yourself. You are EMPOWERED TO CREATE YOUR OWN REALITY. I believe this is helpful information to possess. And yet, why are there so few great traders? I think the answer, quite simply put, is there can be no great success in trading without great commitment, hard work, and sacrifice. I think Walt Whitman said it best when he said, "The whole theory of the universe is directed unerringly to one single individual—namely, to you."

Let me now ask you the all-important question: Why do you want to trade?

This might seem like an odd question to ask; however, I believe it is an important one now that you know how much commitment and sacrifice, not to mention hard work, trading requires. Think for a moment about anything that you ever did in your life that you truly enjoyed, whether it was playing ball when you were a child or going fishing or playing with dolls or trading, for that matter. Consider how important your level of motivation was to the ultimate result of whatever it was that you wanted to accomplish.

It is always very interesting to me to realize how most traders never analyze in any serious way their real motivation for trading. So as you wrestle with this question—Why is it that you want to trade?—it is really important that you "know" the answer. People trade for a variety of reasons—some to enhance their ability to become successful, others to militate against success in profound ways. So it is important that you "know."

Some people trade because for them trading is like what the next vegimatic was for Ralph Cramden. It is, plain and simple, a get-rich-quick scheme. That is not a good reason for trading. For other traders, it is all about excitement, and my attitude is: if that is the primary motivation for your trading, take up skydiving or bungee jumping. Don't trade! It's too dangerous. Save yourself a lot of pain. As you know, trading can be a very painful enterprise. Most of you know exactly what I am talking about.

Another motivation for some traders is that trading becomes a kind of lottery ticket. And this, I believe, is very interesting because, you see, you can lose in trading, but I don't believe you can lose the lottery. I mean, they might not pick your ticket, but psychologically speaking, you don't lose. I make this provocative statement because you know, after you buy that ticket, you are fantasizing where you're going to build your next country house or to which Caribbean island you will sail your new yacht. But for the trader who views trading as a kind of lottery ticket, he can lose in a big way, both psychologically and monetarily.

There are also other motivations. Some trade for entertainment but very soon find themselves playing a leading role in their own real-life docudrama; and there are others who trade just so that they can tell their friends at cocktail parties, "I'm a trader." I have known a lot of traders like that. In fact, consider the man who goes to a physician and complains about having a serious rash on his arm:

The man walks into a doctor's office and shows him a festering rash. The physician examines it and looks perplexed. But he says,

"Take these tablets and come back in a week." The patient follows the doctor's course of treatment but doesn't realize any improvement. The physician, becoming concerned at this point, says, "Use this ointment," and he gives the patient a cream, and at the same time increases the strength of the dosage of the antibiotic. Three weeks pass and the man returns, but there is still no improvement. The physician is now deeply perplexed by all this. He turns to the patient and says, "Let me ask you a question. What do you do for a living?" The man answers matter of factly, "I work at the circus." He continues, "I clean out the stalls of the elephants, and every once in a while I have to give them an enema. I have to reach way, way down deep and . . ." The physician with a radiant look of intuition on his face says, "Well, that is the problem! That is the problem! You have to stop doing that and take up a new line of work. In amazement, the patient looks at the physician and says, "Give up show business?"

You see, for a lot of people, trading is show business. I mean, I know traders who walk into their office and the lights go up and it's like entertainment tonight. So I mention all these things because it is important to know what your motivation is and to remember that your ultimate trading performance will be a direct reflection of the quality and commitment of your motivation to succeed.

Reality

As traders there is one reality that is crucial to act on and that is your reality, your particular point of focus. You must possess an independent-minded attitude that allows you to identify and respond to your reality and realize that all market actions you take emanate from the realization of this reality. It is my belief that whatever we see in the market at any time is purely subjective and in fact our projection, a current reflection of our emotional and physical states. This is not a novel idea. Many others, including Mark Douglas, Charles Faulkner, Bill Williams, and Van Tharp, share a similar point of view. The important point here is to know the difference between an effective (one that works) market reality and one that is an autistic fantasy. Also you must trade from the perspective of your reality to the exclusion of all other points of view.

Many of us think that when we are watching the market (bonds,

S&Ps, soybeans, etc.) we are looking at the same thing, sharing in a common experience. Nothing could be farther from the truth.

We may be looking at the same markets, but we are not seeing the same things. We are not hearing the same thing, and we are not feeling the same thing. Think about anything that you do in "reality." We may all be in the same room, and at that moment in time we all may have a totally different reality. Have you ever walked out on the street after not having a good night's sleep. When that happens, doesn't the world look a little different outside? If you have a toothache, or if you, let's say, lose a boatload of money in the market, things look a little different, don't they? How about when you are in love? Boy, the world really looks good then, doesn't it? The point is, reality is totally based on perspective. So how would that relate to trading? Well, the answer is obvious. You have to understand what your reality is when you are analyzing and trading the market. And you see, as we have learned, our reality of the market is dependent on what is available to us at any given time. The point is, we project our reality. We cannot do otherwise.

Some time ago when I was in Chicago, this point was dramatically brought home to me. I was on an elevator going up to my office, and there was a lady standing next to me who kept staring at my tie. She turned to me and said, "Oh, what a great tie." She then closely inspected the tie. As she was leaving the elevator, she said to me, "They are strawberries, aren't they?" and walked off. I found this interchange most curious because, you see, there were no strawberries—only large, red and blue polar bears—on my tie. I found this very interesting. I said to myself, suppose this woman went into a grocery store and purchased some strawberries, got home, placed them on her kitchen table, and was consumed by a polar bear. That would be a bad batch of strawberries! The funny thing is, that happens in the market all the time. How many times do people see bears when there are "really" only bulls?

Knowing your market reality and consistently applying your proven market strategies, by isolating your particular focus consistently while at the same time feeling good—that is to say, effortless and automatic—is the ultimate key to success.

Many players believe they must do something very special and different on "big" points. As a consequence, players often break from the pattern and style of play that got them to the big point.

Going for too much too early is a strategy breakdown. Going for the low-percentage winner is particularly tempting on the critical points (to get the high-pressure situation over with), but generally spells failure.

Another common way of breaking down strategy-wise on big points is to suddenly start pushing the ball back, hoping your opponent will make an error. Shifting to a very conservative, unaggressive style on the big points in order to keep your errors to an absolute minimum will be about as effective as going for too much too soon. The old dictum, never change a winning game, still holds. Whatever you did to get to the big point, continue doing. As a general rule, you will be most successful if you learn to play offensive, high-percentage tennis on critical points. You become the aggressor and work to get your opponent to make a forced error, without making an error yourself.

To do this, you must know your own game well. Your general strategy for big points should be worked out well in advance of your match. And breaking down is when you don't follow it.

—James Loehr, *The Mental Game,*
Winning at Pressure Tennis (Plume, 1990)

It has been my goal in *The Intuitive Trader* to share everything I have learned and believe about the nature and character of optimum trading performance and how intuition and creativity grow in the fertile ground of mental and physical calm. I base this knowledge on my own successful trading career over many years, my extensive work with high-achieving professional traders, and hundreds of interviews with some of the world's top traders.

I feel extremely fortunate to be able to have a career in a field that provides so many exciting opportunities to learn, although at times painfully, astonishing things about myself and how other traders think and act. It is a constant and exhilarating journey, knowing each day somehow I will be put to a test of my own making, a subtle, almost intangible challenge of calm and control, focus and consistency, awareness and optimism. Each day there will be new things to learn—new insights and understandings.

I know also each day I will call upon skills that have taken me years to acquire, and I will continue to commit myself to learning more about these skills in the future: concentration, attitude, managing pressure, staying motivated, monitoring energy levels, and thinking right. And, I almost forgot, having fun! Each day the same challenge exists to choose excellence and reject what's always easier: mediocrity in trading and everything else in life.

I can't say enough about my enduring love for and fascination with trading. I loved it when I traded on the exchange floor, and I love it today where I trade in an office in front of a screen.

Trading contains much of the comedy and drama of life. In many ways it is a microcosm of life. There is joy, uncertainty, frustration, pain, and struggle. The ultimate test in trading is always to accept the gauntlet of the ultimate challenge: self-control and self-mastery.

It is a continuous process, a transformative process, where the trader can change and be born anew. It involves courage, optimism, and the discipline to succeed—and the intuition that trading does not have to be a scorecard of self-evaluation when it can be a 360-degree universe of self-realization.

The challenge is ours. It is a contest of each trader against himself or herself. Right now, physically calm, mentally relaxed in this moment.

Now, focus.

For Further Reading

Barach, Roland. *Mindtraps: Mastering the Inner World of Investing*. Homewood, IL: Dow Jones-Irwin, 1988.

Baruch, Bernard M. *Baruch: My Own Story*. New York: Holt, Rinehart and Winston, 1957.

Benson, Herbert. *Your Maximum Mind*. New York: Avon, 1987.

———. *Beyond the Relaxation Response*. New York: Times Books, 1984.

———. *The Mind/Body Effect*. New York: Simon & Schuster, 1979.

———. *The Relaxation Response*. New York: William Morrow, 1975.

Berne, Eric. *Intuition and Ego States*. New York: Harper and Row, 1977.

———. "The Nature of Intuition." *Psychiatric Quarterly*, vol. 231, 1949, pp. 203–206.

Board, Richard. "Intuition in the Methodology of Psychoanalysis." *Psychiatry*, vol. 21, 1985, pp. 233–239.

Bronowski, Jacob. *The Origins of Knowledge and Imagination*. New Haven, CT: Yale University Press, 1978.

Butt, Dorcas Susan. *The Psychology of Sport*. New York: Van Nostrand Reinhold, 1976.

Cade, C. M., and N. Coxhead. *The Awakened Mind*. New York: Dell, 1979.

Cootner, P., ed. *The Random Character of Stock Market Prices*. Cambridge, MA: MIT Press, 1964.

Cousins, Norman. *The Healing Heart*. New York: W. W. Norton, 1983.

Czikszentmihalyi, Mihaly. *Flow*. New York: Harper Collins, 1991.

Doboeck, G. J. *Trading on the Edge*. New York: John Wiley and Sons, 1994.

Demark, T. R. *The New Science of Technical Analysis*. New York: John Wiley and Sons, 1994.

Douglas, Mark. *The Disciplined Trader*. New York: New York Institute of Finance, 1990.

Faulkner, Charles, and Lucy Freedman. *NLP in Action*. Chicago: Nightingale Conant, 1993, video tape.

Fisher, Milton. *Intuition*. New York: E. P. Dutton, 1981.

Gallwey, Timothy. *The Inner Game of Tennis*. New York: Random House, 1974.

Gann, W. D. *How to Make Profits Trading in Commodities*. Pomeroy, CA: Lambert-Gann, 1976.

Garfield, Charles A. *Peak Performance: Mental Training Techniques of the World's Greatest Athletes*. Los Angeles: Jeremy P. Tarcher, 1984.

Herrigel, Eugene. *Zen in the Art of Archery*. New York: Pantheon, 1953.

Jacobson, Edmund. *Anxiety and Tension: A Physiologic Approach*. Philadelphia: J. B. Lippincott, 1964.

Jerome, John. *The Sweet Spot in Time*. New York: Avon, 1982.

Jung, Carl Gustar. *Psychological Types*. Princeton, NJ: Princeton University Press, 1971.

King, Winston. *Zen and the Way of the Sword: Arming the Samurai Psyche*. Oxford, England: Oxford, 1990.

Koppel, Robert. *How Winning Traders Think*. Chicago: Chicago Mercantile Exchange, 1995.

———, and Howard Abell. *The Outer Game of Trading: Modeling the Trading Strategies of Today's Market Wizards*. Burr Ridge and New York: Irwin, 1994.

———, and Howard Abell. *High Performance Trading: The Mental Advantage*. Futures Conferences International, 1994. Video Tape Series.

———, and Howard Abell. *The Innergame of Trading: Modeling the Psychology of the Top Traders*. Burr Ridge and New York: Irwin, 1993.

Le Bon, Gustave. *The Crowd: A Study of the Popular Mind*. Atlanta, GA: Cherokee, 1982.

Leonard, George. *Mastery*. New York: E. P. Dutton, 1991.

———. *The Ultimate Athlete*. New York: Viking, 1975.

Loehr, James. *The Mental Game*. New York: Plume, 1990.

———. *Mentally Tough*. New York: Plume, 1986.

———. *Mental Toughness Training for Sports: Achieving Athletic Excellence*. New York: Plume, 1982.

May, Rollo. *The Courage to Create*. New York: W. W. Norton, 1975.

Nideffer, Robert M. *The Inner Athlete*. New York: Crowell, 1976.

Noe, John R. *Peak Performing Principals for High Achievers*. Berkeley, CA: 1984.

Oates, Bob. *The Winner's Edge*. New York: Mayflower, 1980.

Plummer, T. *The Psychology of Technical Analysis*. Chicago: Probus, 1993.

———. *Forecasting Financial Markets: Technical Analysis and the Dynamics of Price*. New York: John Wiley and Sons, 1991.

Poole, Roger. *Toward Deep Subjectivity*. New York: Harper and Row, 1972.

Robbins, Anthony. *Unlimited Power*. New York: Simon & Schuster, 1986.

Schwager, Jack D. *The New Market Wizards: Conversations with America's Top Traders*. New York: Harper Business, 1992.

———. *Market Wizards: Interviews with Top Traders*. New York: New York Institute of Finance, 1989.

Seligman, Martin. *Learned Optimism*. New York: Random House, 1990.

Sperandeo, Victor, with Brown T. Sullivan. *Trader Vic—Methods of a Wall Street Master*. New York: John Wiley and Sons, 1991.

Suzuki, D. T. *Zen Buddism*, ed. William Barrett. New York: Anchor Books, 1956.

Suzuki, D. T. *Zen and Japanese Culture*. Princeton, N.J.: Princeton University Press, 1959.

Toppel, Edward Allan. *Zen in the Markets: Confessions of a Samurai Trader*. New York: Warner, 1992.

Wallas, Graham. *The Art of Thought*. New York: Harcourt Brace, 1926.

Weinberg, Robert. *The Mental Advantage*. Champaign, IL: Leisure Press, 1988.

Williams, Bill. *Trading Chaos*. New York: John Wiley and Sons, 1995.

Winter, Bud. *Relax and Win*. La Jolla, CA: A. S. Barnes, 1981.

Zukav, Gary. *The Dancing Wu Li Masters*. New York: William Morrow, 1979.

About the Author

Bob Koppel is President of Innergame Partners, a proprietary trading and trader execution services division of LFG, LLC, a Chicago-based FCM, clearing all major world exchanges. He is the co-author with Howard Abell of *The Innergame of Trading* (Irwin, 1993) and *The Outer Game of Trading* (Irwin, 1994). He holds advanced degrees in philosophy and group behavior from Columbia University.

Innergame Partners has trained hundreds of traders from all around the globe, including many floor traders who are currently active on the Chicago Mercantile Exchange, Chicago Board of Trade, and Chicago Board of Options. Innergame Partners has over forty years of combined experience as exchange members where they traded successfully for their own accounts. They currently manage the Innergame Trading Portfolio.

For additional information about their services, please contact:
Innergame Partners
Suite 2720
30 South Wacker Drive
Chicago, IL 60606
(312)715-6102
(800)664-1852
(312)715-6133 (fax)

Index